What others are saying about *Got To or Get To?* by Dr

Gary's life and book provide an excellent model for living an intentional life
This book will assist you to live in and enjoy the momer
CLAUDE DOLLINS, Executive Coach, The Dollins Group, Dallas, TX

Gary Schwantz has a unique and uplifting perspective on embracing life and making the most of our journey.
From commonplace, everyday events to those special, once-in-a-lifetime ones, Dr. Schwantz offers wonderful and practical advice on
living your life to the fullest.
JIM COURTNEY, former CEO, University Medical Center, Lubbock, TX

GET TO OR GOT TO? is far more than a self-help or motivational book; its a profoundly wise, articulate, accessible, and deeply
moving meditation on the power that comes from seeing life, love, family, work, pets, heck, EVERYTHING, as a daily gift.
To read it is to exercise the idea of your very existence. on top of all that, it's laugh-out-loud funny.
JOHN BENJAMIN HICKEY, Broadway Actor, New York City, NY

Gary Schwantz is my favorite cornbread Lao-Tsu, and this small book is chock full of the best of his Bubba-Zen.
If you take it to heart, it'll give you a gentle push down that very hard road of living in the moment.
ANDY WILKINSON, Singer, songwriter and poet, Lubbock, TX

Articulate, captivating and funny, this book shows Gary's emotional side as well as his keen insight into life. Always a magnet in a
crowd, Gary is an author, a storyteller, a business and community leader and a devoted friend. Simply told, profoundly true, you will
relate to this book because it shares the genuine, human side to living life fully.
MIRIAM LIEBER, Lieber Consulting, Los Angeles, CA

Wow, this is one powerful little book! I found myself smiling and laughing out loud as Dr. Gary Schwantz described what I now know
to be my very destructive "got to" way of thinking. He not only exposes the wrong attitude of our hearts, he gives us practical and
powerful tools to change the way we think, the way we see, and the way we live every day. You are going to want to get more than
one copy of this book, because when you buy into the "get to" life, those around you are going to want what you have—a life lived to
the fullest, just the way God intended it to be.
KEVIN D. KIRKLAND, Founder and President of Katalyst Ministries
Author of *Broken Walls: And those called to repair them*

Thanks for your book! You have really inspired me to enjoy the moments I have with my 3-year old... We take almost every opportu-
nity that arises =). Today we were invited by a dear friend to join her and her girls at this place called Going Bonkers. It's a HUGE
maze-like, crawl-through, swing-through construction you can crawl through swing through get lost in... lol and you can bet Mommy is
going in with him =) And we have started to ride bikes together as a family.... I am better at it then I thought I would be since it has
been so long!! But I have to admit my backside is a little sore!!
—CARYL CARLISLE

As a college minister, I would love to give this book to every student in my ministry. Whether you are just trying to figure out what you want life to look like, or maybe reconsidering how yours currently looks, Dr. Schwantz provides practical advice that sounds more like a conversation with a friend over coffee than a book. At times serious, at times hilarious, and at times both, I guarantee this book will challenge you to live a more intentional, joyful life.
—TYLER HOLLOWAY, University Minister, The Heights Fellowship, Lubbock, TX

Dr. Gary, we've had the privilege of hearing you in person at several Nite Time and Christmas Decor events. You were life changing then and reading your book was like having you sit down in our living room and just have a heart-to-heart talk with us. This book touches my life in an everyday way, which in turn affects every area of my life, both big and small. This is a book that every member of your family and company should read. Thank you once again, Dr. Gary, for touching our lives in such a wonderful way. This is a book that you GET TO read !!
—JAMEE FOUTS, New Lenox, IL

Gary, I finished your book and wanted to thank you for reminding me what is really important. Driving to work this week, I was thinking that today I will be grateful for something that I normally am not. I am very thankful for my beautiful family, my friends, and my other abundant blessings, but this was different. We had a big snowstorm on Monday and it was bitterly cold. Tuesday morning, the temperature was in the single digits and I was driving my two older children to school. Along the way, I noticed someone outside warming up their car and scraping their windshield. I thought of the book immediately. I was grateful that we have a garage and all of our cars stay warm and dry. This has not always been the case. I thanked God right then and there. I never thought I would be grateful for a garage, but now that I am I will NEVER take it for granted. I gave the book to my lovely wife who reads constantly. I anxiously await her to finish it so we can enjoy life on purpose together. Thanks again.
—Your friend, JACK, HARTFORD, CT

Dr. Schwantz: At the end of your book you ask us to email you, letting you know our thoughts on the book and any impact it may have had. I am not sure how many folks actually do that, but I was inspired. I sent out a special email on Mother's Day this year. Since that email went out, three of the women on that list have opened up to me about my email coming in perfect timing for them, two more called me after not hearing from me in a couple of years. I could write a short story about what's happened with several of those relationships, and how my reading your book has touched their lives. I have lent my copy of your book to the first of five who have asked to read it, and included a CD that includes Eva Cassidy's Somewhere Over the Rainbow cut to go along with the book.
Just a funny little story about another way you impacted my life.....I got in trouble with the Condo Association at my beach house for playing my music too loud one night......I was just doing what you said to do, light's off, lying on the floor, with that song very loud. Have a blessed day.
—CYNTHIA V. MOENCH, CIC, Partner, LRA Insurance, Maitland, Florida

This is a book that is a terrific guide for anyone who has or will be faced with the challenges life will throw at you. I have found Gary's way of looking at daily living to be truly remarkable, so much so that I have presented his book as a gift to my niece and nephews who have graduated high school and now get to make their way on their own, and to my brother-in-law, who at age 50+ has completed his master's degree. Regardless of age, this is a book that will offer you a great deal no matter how many times you read it.

—JOHN ALLMAN, Paso Robles, CA

If you don't continue to grow everyday no matter your age, you will just fade away. This book made me see again the "get to / got to" in my life. At 75, I'm looking forward to another 75, and being able to read and understand the "get to / got to" reasoning will make it happen. Read this book! I DARE YOU. Just starting on my fifth career.

—DON RECTOR, Lubbock, TX

I saw Gary Schwantz do a public speaking engagement where his theme was "Got To or Get To?" and I was transformed immediately into a different frame of mind...a frame of mind and a way of thinking and living life that I try to stay in now (or return to after I have a "got to" day). His book on this theme hammers home the principles that will allow you to enjoy life to its fullest, even in the seemingly mundane everyday tasks and human interactions. By describing personal experiences that everyone can relate to, Gary Schwantz gives a gift that will change your perspective on life.

I hope you "get to" read this book!

—PETER STOREY, Lockport, New York

I found Dr. Gary's narrative style engaging and meaningful. I was unable to put the book down until I had read it from cover to cover. I thank Dr. Gary for this extraordinary book. As a business leader and family man, I found the principles and guidance offered in this book to be invaluable. It's amazing how the same principles apply in our professional lives as they do our personal lives. If we want to be successful as a parent, partner, friend, or professional, we can either do it by leveraging the best of human nature by really listening and taking the time to care, or we can fight it and have worse results and lose the support of others as we proceed. Dr. Gary shows us the right way to conduct business and our lives.

—WILLIAM ELLIOTT, Albuquerque, NM

Dr. Gary has done an outstanding job of simplifying a very complex subject: how to balance your work life with your personal life without compromising those things most important to you. A real gut check on your value system and how it plays into behaviors in all of your life. Great Easy Read—many quotables—great to share with your team (work or pleasure) as a bonding event. Guaranteed at least one "Aha" moment.

—JERRY KNIGHT, Sacramento, CA

GET TO OR GOT TO?

Choosing to love life (or not)

Dr. Gary Schwantz

MAVEN
MARK
BOOKS

Published by MavenMark Books, LLC
www.mwvenmarkbooks.com

Please contact the publisher for quantity discounts for
educational or fundraising purposes.

ISBN: 978-1-59598-073-1
Library of Congress Number: 2008939332

Printed in the United States.

For Janet,

Patrick and Brooke,

Cassidy and Sly,

To Mom, who made my good life possible,

In loving memory of Dad,

and to the Lord who blessed me so with all of them.

ACKNOWLEDGEMENTS

To all my friends who have read or heard portions of this book—thanks for your kind help and encouragement.

It was Kira Henschel who served as my great encourager, editor and ultimately publisher of this book. Thanks for your heart and desire to see this happen.

My friend, Shane Skeens, of Indigo Spin, has been a great help in design and getting the words "just so."

TABLE OF CONTENTS

PREFACE

Can I tell you about my best Thanksgiving ever? First, though, a quick description of my background and my nuclear family ("nu-ku-lar" family, as we say in Texas).

I live in Lubbock, Texas. My Ph.D. is in Family and Consumer Sciences, my other degrees are in family studies and educational administration. I teach at Texas Tech in the College of Human Sciences and fairly recently went out on my own as a speaker, facilitator, author and male model (okay, I exaggerated about the male model part). I've had a variety of careers (what some would call a checkered past I call a well-rounded resume). I've taught and been an administrator at almost all levels of education: high school, community college and at the university level. I've been elected as a

County Commissioner. I have been a carpenter. I've been involved with churches in a variety of ways. Most recently, I spent seven years in corporate education, training and facilitation with a national network of home medical equipment companies. I don't know whether I sound unstable or adventurous, but I will tell you I've had a great time.

More importantly, to the main characters in my life. Janet is my lovely wife of 23 years (23 years of marriage, I don't mean she's 23). She is a speech pathologist, has a wonderful heart. My son, Patrick, is a photographer for a newspaper in San Angelo, Texas. His bride is Brooke, also a photographer. My daughter, Cassidy, is a nursing student at Angelo State, also in San Angelo, Texas. Her husband is Sylvester, Sly for short (and who wouldn't use Sly for short?) By the time you read this, they will have graduated and I hope near enough to see often.

Thanksgiving, three years ago, all of our kids in San Angelo had jobs that required them to either work the night before Thanksgiving or early the morning after. So my wife and I took food down to prepare and serve in my daughter's tiny, one-bedroom apartment (that was before she and Sly became a couple). Cassidy and Patrick invited several friends from school who couldn't go home for the holiday. It so happened that some friends of ours were driving through San Angelo and decided to stop and join us.

All told, there were 17 of us in that apartment. (Did I mention it was a tiny, one-bedroom place?) We sat around a table, a card table, a coffee table, on the arms of the sofa—people were everywhere. The stove was a bit unreliable; its average temperature was just right, 350°F, meaning while the turkey was cooking, the temperature was sometimes 200°F and at times 500°F, so the food came out in phases, not exactly according to plan nor fully done.

We had also forgotten a few items, such as cookie sheets, a carving knife, a cutting board and so did a little makeshift work (we warmed up the rolls on a skillet and carved the turkey with a dinner knife standing upright on a plate). We didn't have enough actual dishes or flatware, so we distributed plastic forks and paper plates.

Sitting there, people hanging from the rafters, eating on any available horizontal surface (and some not so horizontal) with flimsy paper plates collapsing under the weight of underdone turkey and overdone gravy, I realized "THIS IS MY BEST THANKSGIVING EVER!"

People were laughing, having a great time. Our kids were all there—plus additional young people who were grateful to be part of the celebration. Our friends, who are like family to us, simply dove in with the rest. And I thought "What a privilege to be with all these folks."

Let me contrast this to many of my past Thanksgivings. First, I have to lay this out here—my wife and I are a mixed marriage. Janet comes from a family who makes white-bread dressing, stuffed inside the turkey. My family makes dressing the only way that can be considered scriptural—cornbread dressing baked in a pan. For years, when all of our family spent a Thanksgiving together, there was always that battle of the dressings, a battle my wife and I were thrown into whether we liked it or not.

There are simply rules on how holidays are celebrated in each of our families that dictate the right way to do Thanksgiving, which automatically makes all other ways wrong. Throw into the mix the fact that there is always at least one person who gets his or her feelings hurt, someone else who gets angry, etc., etc. Of course, I'm not telling you anything you don't know already. Families are families; we are all insane. Sometimes it works and sometimes it doesn't.

All too often, my holidays haven't felt like privileges at all. Instead, they've felt like obligations, something I do because it is expected, one more thing to get out of the way. By the way, I fully understand my own role in making these holidays difficult at times.

The chaotic, spontaneous and full of life Thanksgiving I shared above got me thinking about my perspectives on life. Most specifically, it got me thinking about the difference between viewing life and its events as an obligation OR viewing life and its events as a privilege: the difference between GOT TO and GET TO.

That difference is vast and is the heart of this book. It is the difference between seeing life as a "GET TO," a privilege, or seeing life as a "GOT TO," one obligation after another.

Here's what I've noticed: no matter the circumstances, even when blessings are abundant, some people simply see all of life as a "GOT TO" —an obligation. Other folks, even when challenges are abundant, see life as a "GET TO" —a privilege.

I do understand that part of the way we see life is a combination of our basic personalities, how we grew up and the experiences we've had. But I don't think those control us. I am convinced that the way we approach life can be intentional.

I think I can choose to see my life as a "GET TO." Actually, I'm convinced you can, too, which is why I wrote this book.

GROWING UP "GOT TO"

I grew up with really good parents. My dad and my best friend in our later years, Richard Leroy Schwantz, died in 1998 and I miss him every day. My mom, Billie Larita Schwantz, still lives and lives well. Good folks, but I grew up in a "GOT TO" home.

As I look back, I realize my dad saw most of his life as an obligation. That made sense. He grew up during the Depression. He served in World War II, came back, married my mom, and had three sons. His generation knew about obligation, duty and honor. Tim Russert, in his book, *Big Russ and Me*, quotes Gail Godwin in describing her dad: "He lived his life by the grace of daily obligations." That was my father. That was his grace.

My dad's challenge was that he had little sense of joy or celebration. It wasn't that he didn't *feel* joy or celebration. What I mean is that he didn't seek those out; his obligations simply came first.

Slight break in continuity here. There was one piece
of life that gave my dad great joy. Janet and I

adopted our daughter Cassidy in 1986. Dad was
never so happy as when Cassidy was small and he
and she would ride around on his lawnmower. It was
that pleasure and experience that told him there
could have been so much more to life, much more
joy.

When we were children, the success of our vacations was measured in miles covered, not places enjoyed. My dad simply loved driving and hated stopping. (I see some of you nodding your heads—you know exactly what I'm talking about). Again, I'm not criticizing him and would do nothing to dishonor my dad. He spent 30 working years selling auto glass. I believe that most of that time, he had only one week of vacation a year. So once a year, the three of us boys and our mom crammed into a station wagon (more specifically a Rambler station wagon—my dad was a Rambler man!) with a mattress in the back and traveled from Texas to Arkansas or Colorado or other nearby states. That could not have been a dream vacation for a man with one week off a year.

When I was eight, we moved out to the country, to a small 20-acre farm. My dad bought it as a hobby, something different to do.

However, even with this farm he bought for relaxation, it seems like most of the time he saw that as an obligation, not as something he would GET TO do when he came home. He always described the farm work as something else he had to do, a GOT TO.

We raised vegetables on our farm and I learned how to can beans and peas and tomatoes. I wish we had viewed it as a good time back then: the pleasure of fresh vegetables and the creativity of canning. Simple food and simple preparation. Instead, I learned to hate canning. It was not something we would GET TO do; my mom saw it as something we have GOT TO do.

We would prepare for canning like we were preparing for war: sterilizing jars; snapping beans and shelling peas; getting the pressure cooker going (and always under the threat of imminent death from it possibly exploding). My mother would be tense, irritable, and exhausted and we three boys would hate every minute. There were always more vegetables to be picked and prepared and canned. The great taste simply wasn't worth all the hassle.

I simply wish every now and then my mom saw canning for the art it was and saw herself as that artist. We never celebrated the food or the process. Again, I'm not being harsh regarding my mom. It was hard work and exhausting. It wasn't a privilege; it was an obligation. I just wished we had been able to see it a different way.

My dad was one of the cheapest men in America (I've inherited that trait). You spent money because you had to; it was an obligation to earn money and an obligation when you spent it. Even though my parents worked and sacrificed to give us boys the best possible Christmases, I wish they had enjoyed them more. We didn't GET TO set the Christmas tree out and put up decorations; that was something Mom and Dad saw as a GOT TO. Mom didn't GET TO shop for gifts, it was a GOT TO (though I am proud to note that today, she has become much more thoughtful in the gifts she gives and seems pleased to be able to find gifts that we really like).

Even our approach in the church—-perhaps especially our approach to church—was a GOT TO. Going to church was some-thing you're supposed to do. We sang *Amazing Grace*. It just seemed like we didn't often believe the "grace" part of it (and weren't dramatically enthralled with the "amazing" part, either!) That said, there were some great folks in that church who did understand grace and the privilege of faith. And, in fact, they saved my heart as a kid.

I don't remember my folks talking much about enjoying the church where we were. In fact, I remember more vividly their frustrations. However, church was supposed to feel like that, something you were obligated to. You didn't willy-nilly change churches, looking for one you liked! You stuck it out.

> How many of you who grew up in small (or large churches) can identify with this point? You heard couples share "inspiring" messages about their marriages, how making a marriage succeed is work 24 hours a day, 7 days a week, but by the grace of God, they've stayed together. Those aren't people who GET TO be married, those are people who see marriage as an obligation, something they've GOT TO do.

THE DARK SIDE

So, why am I telling you all of this? It is to make the point that I am an original member of the Dark Side. I'm not one of those people who is naturally content with life. My nature is to see life as an obligation and not to expect the best out of it. My nature is to know that every silver lining has a dark cloud behind it.

Dr. Gary Schwantz

I don't know if "goober" is a technical term you understand, but know that at 16, I was a major "goober." And know that my nature is still that of a 16-year-old kid with braces and terrible skin and limited expectations about life being good today.

The reason I'm the right person to discuss how to see life as a GET TO and not a GOT TO is because I have to work so freakin' hard at it. I have to remind myself to view life as a privilege, every single day! I have had to consciously devise and follow principles to keep my dark side submerged and my "sunny" side up.

As I look back, there are two primary impacts that worked against this dark side. The genesis of this realization that life can be a GET TO actually came about when I was a kid, my first summer working at a summer camp in the hill country of Texas. I was 19 years old. I don't even know why a kid like me, self-conscious, shy, lacking any kind of confidence whatsoever, thought he could work at a camp. Actually, as I think about it, it was obligation that drove me. At the time, I thought I was headed into the ministry, so I imagined it would be an experience that would help prepare me for my life's path.

Instead, that summer and several thereafter, I learned some new freedoms about celebration and life. There was an interesting freedom at camp among the kids; their faith in God seemed to free them, rather than bind them. Getting to know these folks, their kind acceptance of me— a major goober—had a great impact.

However, let me tell you what else had a great impact: a little book that one of the directors there gave me at the beginning of the summer. It was a simple, small book, *Celebrate the Temporary*, written by Clyde Reid and published in 1972. That little book talked about noticing what we eat and celebrating relationships and leaning into our pain.

I took those simple messages to heart, with encouragement of some lovely people. Dr. Reid's little book continues to be a reminder to me to this day. My intention for the little book you're holding in your hands is that it will serve the same purpose: a reminder that we can choose life as a privilege, a GET TO.

The second primary impact on lightening up my dark side is this: I simply married well. My wife Janet is self-confident, content with life, and it IS her nature to be "sunny." Early on, when Janet and I and our children, Patrick and Cassidy, went on vacations, I tried my dad's approach and tried to measure vacations by miles driven. My lovely wife, in a tone that still scares me, said "unh-uh." Janet taught me quickly a different way to measure the success of vacations—by moments enjoyed. I learned the best parts of vacations actually tend to occur at roadside parks and on those roads less traveled.

I, the cheapest man in America, who had learned that gifts are bought when required, married a woman who buys gifts for others for no significant reason, and spends money to do so. I still struggle with what seems to go against the universe, nature and scripture, but she is slowly winning me over, year by year.

I, who spend the first six months of any job hoping to find a different one, married a women who loves what she does (Janet is a speech pathologist) then leaves it at the hospital instead of waking up at 5:00 in the morning thinking about it. How can that be normal?

I, a former died-in-the-wool GOT TO guy, am an unapologetically, irritatingly, but still with a huge Dark Side, GET TO guy.

My biggest GET TO? I get to love my wife!

For those of you for whom life has always been a GET TO, you may not see this as a significant progression. But for those of us who prefer (or at least are more comfortable with life on the Dark Side), it is significant and not so easy.

TO THE PRESENT

As I'm writing this little book, my wife and I are at a good point in our lives. Our son Patrick is a photojournalist, married to a wonderful young lady named Brooke, whom I will admit to being madly in love with. Our daughter Cassidy and Sly were married a few months ago, in a beautiful ceremony, and they are in the wonderful struggle that all married college students find of limited money and time.

Today, just Janet and I share a house that we love. We also share that house with two greyhounds we also love, despite their bad breath, shedding and failure to understand "sit," "stay," or "get that out of your mouth."

My life is full and fairly easy, but there are too many times where I seem to have a vague sense of discontent—nothing dramatic —but I don't breathe in life the way I want to. So it is on those mornings that I have to consciously remind myself to "savor" this life today. Unlike my too-consistently-content wife, I have to decide to make my life different and full and conscious—today.

I desire to remind myself that I want to savor not just the extraordinary, I also want to savor the ordinary. I want to notice my wife's smile and scent. I want to take in the common blackbirds, right now, that for some reason have chosen my birdbath for their Saturday night party. I want to be able to taste the food I eat and smell the smells I smell (I love that line!) and feel the pains and pleasures of life—today.

This is not a book about leaving it all behind and finding a new life. Others write about their chances to savor life at the tops of mountains or across deserts or in a jungle. I do want some mountaintop experiences (I love having something to look forward to), but I actually live the majority of my life at home and at work and in traffic and in my yard. That's where I want to experience life more fully. I don't want to wait until I'm somewhere else. I want to savor life today—without having to feel like it involves a trek across the ocean (or the desert).

This is a book about finding life where I have it. You know what I want to do? I want to mow my lawn and experience the smell of the grass and the feel of the hot sun on my shoulders and know that life is good. I do want adventure, for I know how much God created my heart for adventure. I want some risk and uncertainty. But I also want that living of life to involve my family and friends and common, everyday thoughts.

The following pages contain the simple words I use to remind myself how to do that: to savor life where I find it and when I find it, to see life as a GET TO.

You will find in these pages reminders to what I believe are the keys for those who love life:

- They do it on purpose
- They notice the moments
- They celebrate and have fun
- They let go
- They are grateful
- They take time

THOSE WHO LOVE LIFE...
DO IT ON PURPOSE

Why is it some people seem so full of life? Why is it they always seem to have something to look forward to and great memories to share? I think it is because they intend it. They choose it.

This first key to savoring life is *intentionality*. It means living life on purpose. It means deciding that today is the day I notice. It's this simple: if we want to savor life, we have to notice it. We have to decide we will be a part of it. We will turn off the TV, open the door to the outside and get our bony protuberances out and experience life.

Stephen Covey, in his book *The Seven Habits of Highly Effective People*, makes an excellent point regarding choices. He contends that what makes us different from animals is our ability to choose. Animals simply react to stimuli. When my dogs and I go for a walk and they see a squirrel, they don't think "You know, each time we do this, we never get the squirrel because we are on leashes. Perchance we should pass on this one." No, they go after the squirrel, despite the leashes and the sudden stop at the end!

On the other hand, I have the choice in how I react to stimulus. I drive a little Miata, a small convertible. On a good day driving, Marvin Gaye on the radio, sun shining, no rush to get anywhere— someone cuts me off—no problem. In my mildest voice (or at least my mildest thoughts), I state, "Go in peace, my brother." However, on a bad day driving, when I'm in a rush and the music is bad and it's hot and dusty (more on living in West Texas later) and someone cuts me off—now I'm upset. If I'm in a bad enough mood, I might choose to go on a reconnaissance mission and track the other driver down so he or she knows exactly how upset I am—and once I accomplish that, the fact that the other driver doesn't care how upset I am, makes me even more upset so that my day starts off bad and gets worse …

Sorry, I lost track for a moment there. See, same occurrence, yet different reactions. I know there are outside circumstances that color my perspective, but the fact is Covey is right: I choose my reactions and that choice determines the rest of the day.

META-AWARENESS

I also choose how to notice life. I call this "meta-awareness." In our context, it simply means "being aware of being aware," which will make sense in a moment. Meta-awareness means I have the choice to step back and see myself from a different perspective.

No one hates stop lights (notice I don't call them traffic lights—they are STOP lights) more than I do. I am not a very patient person. I can choose to be frustrated (usually my first choice). But when I am rational—meta-aware—I step back and review. "Let's see. I'm in my car, the top is down, I have music playing, what's the rush?"

Back to the theme of the book: Meta-awareness is realizing I GET TO be in a car with the top down (how many people would love to be able to do that?), I GET TO drive, I GET TO listen to music.

Meta-awareness means that I can be eating and notice that I'm not tasting my food. By choice, I can choose to savor the tastes and the smells! I can be with my wife and notice that I'm not paying close attention and change my perspective (before she changes it for me).

I'll try not to use the term "meta-awareness" too many more times because it sounds vaguely like I should be dressing in a mohair parka and chanting in a pyramid with crystals of various strengths. But this concept goes to the heart of this book. More than anything, savoring life is consciously choosing to notice. It is:

- when I'm not being grateful, it is reminding myself to count my blessings;
- when I'm moving too fast, it is reminding myself to slow down;
- when I'm too comfortable in my routine, it is reminding myself to shake it up.

Does this meta-awareness stuff make sense to you? It is me telling myself "I am going to be aware of how I react to life and to my choices." Give it a try. The reality is that those who experience life do it intentionally, on purpose.

Actual Physiological Support
for Schwantz's Ramblings

There are two primary structures in the brain to consider. The neocortex makes up the majority of our brain – it's kind of the top layer. It is within the neo-cortex that we learn technical skills and process most of the data we receive. Deeper within the brain is the basal ganglia. It is actually a more primitive part of the brain; it does not act as quickly as the neo-cortex and it takes more work to process and store informa-tion (honest—look it up!).

Interestingly enough, the basal ganglia is the seat of our emotions. When I talk about meta-awareness, I really am talking about processing through the basal ganglia. This means attaching our emotions to what we see. We go beyond the "seeing" of the neo-cortex and begin "observing." We respond with our emotions and memories, much as we do to certain music or smells. Is that cool or what?

LIVING WITH THE BRAKES ON

Another part of living life intentionally is being willing to take some risks, to get outside our comfort zone. I'm not necessarily talking about taking physical risks. However, if for you fully experiencing life means jumping out of airplanes or into crocodile pits, I'm with you. In fact, I like the idea of taking crocodiles skydiving, but perhaps I'm getting off the subject here.

> Actually, skydiving does come to mind, because among my mid-life crisis friends is one who has taken up skydiving. Can I tell you a secret about him? Skydiving is no risk for him; what he won't risk right now is loving his wife or their daughters. It's easier for him to skydive (or walk across hot coals with Anthony Robbins or travel all of the time) than it is to risk that type of vulnerability.

I think there are two primary reasons we avoid risk (in addition to the fact that it is natural we do so). The first is simply because it involves effort and we prefer life be easier, not better.

Many people are stuck where they are, but it's not because they are incompetent and it's not because of circumstances and it's not because of a lack of opportunity. It is simply because it involves turning the TV off, getting up out of our recliners and trying new things.

The second is simply fear. I call it "living with the brakes on," but let me see if I can describe my thoughts effectively. Lubbock, Texas, is both a center for medical facilities and an aging population and the home of Texas Tech University with about 27,000 students.

WE PREFER LIFE TO BE EASIER, NOT BETTER!

The speed limit on the majority of our main streets is 40 mph. Students, being who they are, drive an average of 60; older people, especially those heading for a doctor's appointment, drive an average of 17. Me, I drive the only appropriate speed—46 mph. The main street I drive most days carries both students headed to Tech and older people headed for medical care. There are numerous side streets that come into this main avenue. What I've noticed in following some of the older people is that, out of fear, they brake at every block where side streets intersect with this main street. They don't come to a full stop, but simply tap on the brakes as they pass each side street. Every few seconds, each time they pass a street, they are preparing for the worst to happen. I know they think they are being safe and I understand their fear and often their confusion. However, these folks are actually creating dangers for everyone else driving.

(I'm trying to grow here. You have probably already noted that I am not a patient driver and I've been too harsh in my mind with these folks, until I remember that they are older and often sick and scared and unfamiliar with the territory as they try to find doctor's offices and clinics and hospitals. That is meta-awareness at work— reminding myself not to be harsh or judgmental.) Of course, approaching that age so rapidly helps too!

This is related specifically to my life on the dark side. Not a perfect analogy, but living with the brakes on means spending my life expecting the worst to happen. It reminds me of the most pessimistic phrase I remember: "Someone told me cheer up, it could be worse. So I cheered up and sure enough, it got worse."

Living with the brakes on means never quite abandoning ourselves to life. One of the assignments I've given in the past to my students at Texas Tech was called a "Wisdom Assignment." They were to interview folks over 35, asking their regrets, their dreams and their best advice. Several times the "best" advice boiled down to this: "Don't get your hopes up and you'll never be disappointed." That is a soul-wringing approach to life. Living with the brakes on means not getting your hopes up. That's safe and almost risk-free, other than the risk of never experiencing a fullness to life.

> To savor life sometimes, we just have to do things we're not sure of, we need to be outside our comfort zone. We need the tension to feel fully alive.

LIVE FREELY, RECKLESSLY, IN FIRST DRAFTS!

Brenda Ueland published a book in 1938 that I happened to pick up off the shelves of our local library one day. I thought it was a book about writing, since the title is *If You Want to Write*. Actually, her book should be entitled *If You Want to Live*. As you read the following quotes from her book, consider her to be speaking of living rather than writing:

- Know that you have talent, are original and have something important to say.

- Know that it is good to work. Work with love and think of liking it when you do it. It is a privilege.

- Tackle anything you want to—novels, plays, anything.

- Don't fret or be ashamed of what you have written in the past.

Remember the great line from the movie *Finding Forrester*, in which an older author is teaching a young man to write. The young man asks what the secret to writing is. Forrester's answer: "The secret to writing is to write."

The Ueland quote that sticks with me, beyond everything else, is this: *Write freely, recklessly, in first drafts*!

Allow me to restate "Live freely, recklessly, in first drafts." That sentence has two meanings for me. The first is this. As I am writing this, I have an unfortunate tendency to edit myself. I remember a sentence I didn't like and I go back to correct it. I think of something that should be deleted in the introduction; there's a better story I could add. Instead of just writing and flowing and then coming back, I tap on the brakes while I write and it kills the flow.

The greater meaning is this: Life is a first draft. As a kid, I thought there was a time I would be grown and knowledgeable and competent and know exactly what I was doing. As a parent, there was a time I thought I would be grown and competent and know exactly what I was doing. In my field of work, there was a time I thought I would be grown and competent and know exactly what I was doing.

LIFE IS A FIRST DRAFT.

I was wrong, I am wrong. Life is a first draft. We do the best we can. For me, being free and reckless doesn't mean driving 90, abandoning my marriage or selling everything to live on a boat. Instead, it is the freedom to love my wife and children with reckless abandon. It is the freedom to throw myself into projects or music or food. It is worrying less about what others think.

A psychotic aside:

I sound so assured, don't I? Let me tell you a bit about myself. All I need to be satisfied with life are these three things:

- Be good at everything I do.
- Make no mistakes, ever.
- Have everyone like me, love me, adore me.

As long as I have all of those things, I'm completely satisfied.

ADVENTURE APPLIED

Here is a story I think explains this concept of "life is a first draft" in terms that are understandable to us all.

Helen (not her real name) works in the curriculum development for one of the departments at Texas Tech University where I teach. Among our last conversations was something like this:

"Helen, how ya' doing?

"Gary, I'm doing fine.

"Are you enjoying your job?"

"No, it sucks the life out of me."

"Have you thought about finding another one?"

"No, I'm going to stick this out to retirement.

"Really? How much longer?"

"Seven years!"

Seven years! Lifetimes are lived in seven years! We can go through almost two presidential terms in seven years. The world can change completely in seven years.

Helen and I visited for a little bit longer, and she revealed that actually, she would like to work in a gift shop. For a while, she talked about how she would like life to be, but eventually she rationalized back around to reasons to stay where life is set and secure (easier but not better). She made the point that another job could have all the same problems; she likes some of the folks she works with; it could be worse. Her primary point was this—she will be fully vested in seven years. When she retires, fully vested, she and her husband would like to buy an RV and see the country. That's when they will really enjoy life. End of conversation with Helen.

Another colleague, Rosa (her real name!) used to work with me. Rosa and her husband divorced when her daughter was very young and Rosa raised that wonderful daughter by herself. Rosa had gotten her daughter through college and now into grad school. So her situation was this: she had a comfortable and secure job where we both worked. She had found a very comfortable town home with a really nice patio here in Lubbock. Life was easy.

But Rosa had a dream to have a used bookstore and started talking about moving to Post, a little town 45 minutes from Lubbock. In Post she found a location, in one of the classic buildings downtown that are narrow and deep and have a room above, in which she could create the bookstore downstairs and live upstairs, on a month-to-month lease (and for next to nothing). Her plan was to open the bookstore on weekends and special events. She would keep working here with us in Lubbock during the week.

> Post has one of those little downtowns that should have died here in West Texas, but they found a way to keep it alive. It has an active community theatre that draws in folks from the area and the old hotel is now a bed & breakfast. There are a couple of gift shops, a small museum, and a little arts studio.

Well, anyone with any sense could have told her it wouldn't work; she wasn't going to make a living with a used bookstore in Post, Texas. "Think of how much more you are going to spend in gas." "What happens if it snows; how will you get to work?" Others made the excellent points that the timing wasn't right, why not wait and save a little money, enjoy Lara being on her own, relax on that nice patio!!!!

Rosa took what I think is a nice, classic, decision-making approach. "If I do this and it doesn't work, what's the worst that could happen?" The answer: get rid of the books, find another nice town home with a patio in Lubbock. "What's the worst that could happen if I don't do this?" The answer: Life continues, things are okay, but I will wonder what I could have done.

Rosa took the only rational approach: she followed her heart instead of everyone else's advice. And I will tell you, they were right. Rosa's not going to make a living having a used bookstore in Post, Texas. However, what she has made, is a life.

First, Rosa's natural artist has thrived. Her job with us often killed that artistic spirit; her bookstore lifts it. She has special book signings and events. Rosa herself is writing again and produced her first play.

Second, she has found a way to make a little extra income. She gets the books on consignment from another used book dealer, so she has no huge investment in inventory. She sells quite a few around special events. And she's started selling books on-line.

Third! Because of Rosa's involvement in Post, I got to know some of the folks there and as a result, was invited to a wedding there not too long ago. The groom's name was James; he is a retired Methodist minister with a great heart for ministry and encouragement and affection. James' wife had left him while he was pastoring the church there in Post, a little over 4 years ago. However, James met a wonderful woman who was creative and funny and adventurous. He decided to fall in love again. That day, the bride was beautiful; she was beaming and floating and excited. The only one at that wedding who couldn't see the bride was Rosa – because she was that bride. (But you knew that already, didn't you?)

Rosa didn't go to Post to find love, she went to find a small adventure. Instead, she found a great adventure, far beyond her wildest dreams, simply because she was willing to take a small step, to take some risks. Rosa has chosen to write her own story, creating and re-creating that first draft every day.

I can't get around this one: the core of savoring life seems to be found somewhere within our willingness to take some risks. Notice how short Helen's story above is? Her next seven years are set: she has a job she can complain about while she waits to get vested and puts her life on hold, all on the hope that she and her husband both stay alive and healthy and get their RV. I hope they do, with all my heart I do.

Rosa's story? She's busy writing it every single day!

Those who love life do it on purpose—they GET TO write their own stories.

APPLICATION—DO IT ON PURPOSE

At the end of each chapter, you will notice these sections with questions and ideas. I do hope you will study each question, write your answers, and share them with someone else.

What is one thing you are avoiding doing, either because it's messy or it involves you getting out of your chair?

One thing that I think I would like to do this evening, even though it would take some effort, would be to

One thing that I think I would like to do this weekend, even though it would take some effort, would be to

What is one adventure you've thought of doing, but continue putting it off (it doesn't have to be big) or one thing you would like to learn to do that scares you a little?

SOME IDEAS!

- Call the continuing education division at your local college to see if they are offering a course soon in something that interests you (notice you don't have to sign up yet, just get the catalog).

- Rent a convertible for the day.

- Take your daughter, your son, your wife or husband, out for dinner, just the two of you.

- Share with someone the thing you've always wanted to do, but have been afraid to try.

- Go to a restaurant you don't know to try food you're not sure of.

- Take a train (if one is nearby—shoot, even if it's not nearby— same goes for a roller coaster.

- Find a drive-in movie, pop some popcorn and take lawn chairs and enjoy. Www.drivein.com has a fairly current list of drive-ins arranged by state.

- Go to a play, to a concert, walk an art trail.

- Take your dogs for a walk. If you don't have dogs, borrow someone else's.

- Set up a Slip-n-Slide® in your yard.

THOSE WHO LOVE LIFE ...
...NOTICE THE MOMENTS

think this may be the piece of this book that is the easiest to write about and the hardest to live. I like the word immediacy— it simply means "being in the moment." You already know what I mean—but allow me the privilege of a little elucidation (actually, I was just looking for a reason to use the word "elucidation").

Savoring life, at its best, is done in the moment. I will talk about living in the past in the next chapter—let's talk here about our unfortunate tendency to live our lives in the future. Every semester, I get to teach about 400 college students. Most of my students are seniors, close to graduation. Many of them see my class simply as a barrier that must be overcome to get to graduation. That's too bad, because we actually get to discuss quite a few cool things and though I can't recommend the instructor very highly, the topics are great.

Those students are living for six months from now—graduation —and they have stopped noticing today. In fact, this life of living in the future began long ago, always waiting for one more thing to happen before choosing to be happy or to fully experience life. See if you recognize yourself in the partly autobiographical (and partly hypothetical) descriptions below:

LIVING IN THE FUTURE

- When I was 5, I couldn't wait to get to go to real school and ride the big yellow bus.

- When I learned to print, I couldn't wait to learn to write cursive, like the big kids.

- When I was in Junior High, I couldn't wait to be in High School (okay, that part's rational. We all need to be out of Junior High).

- When I was a freshman, I couldn't wait to be 16 and get my driver's license—give me some wheels and finally I'll own this world. Then I will enjoy life!

- Once I got my license, I couldn't wait to graduate and go to college and life would be full.

- Once in college, I couldn't wait until Christmas break, spring break and summer.

- Once part way through college, I couldn't wait to graduate and for real life to begin and get my first real job —Real life, that's what I need!

- Once real life began, I couldn't wait to get a better job.

- With real life, also came the need to find a serious girlfriend, so I couldn't wait to find a girlfriend.

- A few weeks later, I couldn't wait to find a better girlfriend.

- What I then needed was to get married. I wasn't married, so that was why I wasn't enjoying life as much as I should.

- Once married, we need to have children.

- We need to get our children out of diapers and into pre-school. That's when life will start getting better.

- We need a bigger house and a better car. I think that's what will make the difference.

- If we can get the kids out of junior high and high school...when that date comes, life really begins.

- Once the kids are in college and away, and my wife and I have some time for each other, that's when life will finally hit its peak.

- I wonder if I need a different wife? We don't talk much. I don't think she appreciates me.

- I think that promotion will be the crowning piece. Sure, I'm not very happy now, but I think it's just a matter of time. I'll earn quite a bit of money then, making it easier to retire.

- In fact, maybe I can retire early and really enjoy life. That's when it will all be worth it. That's when I will be happy.

- Retirement is okay, but what we really need is that RV we've talked about, and new golf clubs, and maybe create a shop in my garage.

- I think what we really need is a bigger RV and to see our kids (and especially our grandkids) more often. That's when I'm going to really enjoy life, on those weekends when I can see my grandkids.

- You know what? Here's when I'm going to enjoy life— when I'm dead!

I wish this were exaggeration instead of a valid description of how many people live their lives, always waiting for something to happen for them to enjoy life, finally. In the meantime, they miss it. They miss the pleasure of their successes. They miss their kids growing up. They miss the chance to love their wives and their friends. They miss the chance to taste the food they eat and savor the scent of life.

LIFE IS LIVED IN THE MOMENTS

You know that life is lived in the moments. It is the choice to be there. I notice that all of my best memories are situated in the moments of life. To be frank, most of the family vacations I tried so hard to plan and holidays and big events we pointed to—they were usually disasters. My life's fullness instead has been in conversations at bedtime and at a roadside park. It's time together in the car or in the backyard or walking the dogs. I'm not skilled at a lot of things, but I will tell you this. I have worked to structure my life and my career to be there for the moments—to enjoy my family and friends and food. I've not always been good at it, but I've at least been aware.

Life is best lived when I *choose* to notice it. It goes back to my very first point: those who love life do it *on purpose*. I am, I will be, purposeful about noticing life. That means when something attracts me—a beautiful sunrise, a storm in the distance, a bird nearby—I stop and notice and really take it in.

I work to take the time to notice geese flying overhead and watch full moons rise. I've savored the 3-year-old girl who became 21. I've inhaled the little boy who now takes pictures for a living and is a wonderful husband to his lovely wife. I spent the time talking to my dad over the fence for those many years before he passed away. I still learn something new about my wife—I think I know her hair and face and figure and yet am still surprised.

In a Sunday School class of young couples I teach, I know this week, one of my young men is considering a job that will pay extremely well— much better than what he makes now. It will involve significant time on

the road and many nights away from home. The
thing is, I've never known any man who loves his new
daughter more. I understand ambition as well as any
one. I know his greatest desire is to make a great life
for his family—and the money would help. My prayer
for him is simply that he make the right decision.
Those baby girls aren't baby girls for long.

Life is lived in the moments. I am surrounded by those who live
constantly for tomorrow—for that time they have enough money and
time to enjoy life; when every problem will be solved and they will
be able to focus on the good things of life. I fear it will never happen
for them.

Enjoy the moments, a moment at a time. Be here—right now.

LIFE IS MESSY

I've already made the point that we often choose what is easiest
rather than what is best. And being intentional in experiencing life
makes life better, but it doesn't make it easier. I mentioned my two
greyhounds earlier. Faith is the tan one, Onyx is the black one.

Greyhounds do what any large dogs do; they leave large gifts in the backyard. Faith has created a figure-8 race track in my backyard —so there are areas where it's useless to try to grow anything. At times Faith's breath is so bad that it brings tears to your eyes (and peels paint off doors). They both shed, so if I wear white clothes, then Onyx's remnants show; if I wear dark clothes, Faith's.

For any number of reasons, they seem to have an urgency to go outside each morning about 4:15. I sleep on my side, my face out, so my face is exactly of the level of theirs and they notify me of their desire to go outside with a seriously wet kiss (depending on the dream at the time, it offers an interesting end). We have to feed and water and walk them. When we travel, we have to find someone to take care of them. They're trouble, no doubt about it, and my life would be easier without them.

My life would be easier—but it would not be better. And I will tell you why. Because when I come home from a hard day or a long trip, those dogs welcome me home by allowing me to sit on their couch and then each wraps herself around me, trying to get as close as humanly possible (actually, as close as caninely possible). My heart rate and my respiration slow and I begin to relax. If they could figure out how, they would put their arms around my neck and ask me if I've had a good day. They're messy and they don't make my life easier, but I wouldn't live without them. They turn my life from okay to best.

The ultimate recognition of life being messy is the decision to have children. Do you want worry and frustration and hurt? Have a child. Do you want a life that is full and rich and challenging? Have a child. My son and his lovely wife struggle at times to get by on what they make. My daughter, just recently married, is working to finish nursing school and stress and worry are high. Life would be easier without them to worry about—but it would be so much less fulfilling and meaningful.

DON'T WAIT

For a long time it had seemed to me that life was about to begin--real life. But there was always some obstacle in the way, something to be gotten through first, some unfinished business, time still to be served, a debt to be paid. Then life would begin. At last it dawned on me that these obstacles were my life.
— Dr. Alfred Sous

I love this point from Dr. Sous. In visiting with friends, it seems there is always one more thing they need to get out of the way (their obligations—their GOT TOs) before they really will enjoy life—get school paid off or a project handled or get in better shape. I fear that if they wait to get every issue cleared up, if they wait to clean up every mess, they will never get around to the GET TO parts of life. .

Don't wait to clean up all your messes before you start enjoying life. Don't wait to get totally out of debt or completely healthy or without responsibilities. Live it now. My encouragement—don't take the easy way, take the best way.

> Maya Angelou said it well about life seeming to love those who choose to live it:
> *Because of the routines that we follow, we often forget that life is an ongoing adventure. We leave our homes for work, acting and even believing that we will reach our destinations with no unusual event startling us out of our set expectations. The truth is we know nothing, not where our cars will fail or when our buses will stall, whether our places of employment will be there when we arrive, or whether, in fact, we ourselves will arrive well and alive at the end of the*

journey. Life is pure adventure, and the sooner we realize that, the quicker we will be able to treat life as art: to bring all our energies to each encounter, to remain flexible enough to notice and admit it when what we expected to happen did not happen. We need to remember that we are created creative and can invent new scenarios as frequently as they are needed.

Life at its essence boils down not to one season at a time or one day at a time. Life at its essence boils down to celebrating one moment, noticing that moment and savoring it. Now is the moment. Those who love life notice the moments. They GET TO experience life every day.

WAIT, I REMEMBERED SOMETHING: PAIN!

When I picture people writing books, I imagine that they are doing so in their study, flooded by sunlight, a nice spot of tea at the desk. Well, the reality is that books are written where they are written. As I write these words, I am sitting on a patch of carpet at Dallas-Fort Worth airport where another flight of an airline that will remain unnamed (it does rhyme with Lamerican Lairlines) is delayed, once again. I don't know why, but I am reminded that another reason we avoid risk (and a lot of the other things I will discuss through this book) is our fear of pain.

We try so hard, we are encouraged by advertising, we spend enormous amounts of money—to avoid pain! Listen, I don't like pain, but it is such a big part of life. I opened my life to pain when I decided to become a husband and father. I opened my life to pain when I chose to age. I opened my life to pain by choosing to be alive.

I don't seek out pain, but I know that growth can't occur without it. I had ACL replacement surgery on my knee last year. I wish it was because of a lifetime of strenuous athletic achievement, but it's nothing so exciting or honorable as that. It simply seems that those ligaments gradually disappeared sometime over the last decade. I went through a bit of rehab on the knee. I had a great therapist who would get me in a position where it was painful, then help me push just a hair more. My nature, as soon as I hit a painful spot, was to back off. My therapist helped me move beyond that point.

I learned I could handle more pain than I thought, primarily by learning into it. We can handle more pain than we are aware. I'm not encouraging us to seek it out, but I often see people who simply can't risk pain, so they:

- choose not to date again after a hard break-up or divorce.
- choose not to interview again after the disappointment of not getting the job they wanted.
- basically give up on their kids because they've been hurt one too many times.
- give up at 1K into a 5K race.

There is an interesting collection of letters from the early 1900s. The author of the letters was Rainer Maria Rilke, and the collection is now called *Letters to a Young Poet*. He writes a series of letters in response to a young poet and student at military school struggling with his art and his isolation and his life. I quote a piece he writes here:

> You have had many sadnesses, large ones, which
> passed. And you say that even this passing was
> difficult and upsetting for you. But please, ask yourself
> whether these large sadnesses haven't rather gone
> right through you.

Perhaps many things inside you have been transformed; perhaps somewhere, deep inside your being, you have undergone important changes while you were sad.

The only sadnesses that are dangerous and unhealthy are the ones that we carry around in public in order to drown them out with the noise; like diseases that are treated superficially and foolishly, they just withdraw and after a short interval break out again all the more terribly; and gather inside us and are life, are life that is unlived, rejected, lost, life that we can die of.

If only it were possible for us to see farther than our knowledge reaches, and even a little beyond the outworks of our presentiment, perhaps we would bear our sadnesses with greater trust than we have in our joys.

For they are the moments when something new has entered us, something unknown; our feelings grow mute in shy embarrassment, everything in us withdraws, a silence arises, and the new experience, which no one knows, stands in the midst of it all and says nothing.

Read that piece again—sadnesses do not pass, "instead ask yourself whether these large sadnesses haven't rather gone right through you." Our sadnesses and our pain do go right through us; they change our lives because "something new has entered us." I don't know how we grow without pain.

If you are like me, a parent, I never want my kids to experience pain. When their jobs disappoint them or they don't do well in school or they have a fight with their spouse or when someone hurts their feelings, I want to make that hurt go away immediately. I want to protect them—which is obviously the best way to keep them from growing. I know by our nature we tend to work to avoid pain or struggle. We choose comfort, we choose that which is easier instead of better. Have you seen the movie *Little Miss Sunshine?* Here's a great scenario from it. Dwayne is in high school; Frank is his slightly bizarre uncle:

> **Dwayne**: I wish I could just sleep until I was eighteen and skip all this crap- High school and everything— just skip it.
> **Frank**: You know Marcel Proust?
> **Dwayne**: He's the guy you teach.

Frank: Yeah. French writer. Total loser. Never had a real job. Unrequited love affairs. Gay. Spent 20 years writing a book almost no one reads. But he's also probably the greatest writer since Shakespeare. Anyway, he uh... he gets down to the end of his life, and he looks back and decides that all those years he suffered, Those were the best years of his life, 'cause they made him who he was. All those years he was happy? You know, total waste. Didn't learn a thing.

So, if you sleep until you're 18... Ah, think of the suffering you're gonna miss. I mean high school? High school—those are your prime suffering years. You don't get better suffering than that.

I wish I could say this better: embrace your pain—it is more evidence that you and I are alive and experiencing life.

One piece comes to mind that has been such an encouragement for me regarding this book. My publisher and great encourager for this book, Kira, helps take care of her elderly and ill mother. She has really structured her life around being able to care for her mother, out of a sense of love more than a sense of duty. After reading the initial manuscript, Kira discussed how she sees taking care of her mom as a GET TO—a privilege. Even when it's felt like an obligation, she's been able to remind herself of the privilege and honor. I know she hates the pain for her mom and feels the pain herself—but she's chosen to understand it as a part of their lives together. What could be just words Kira has chosen to make come alive.

APPLICATION:

THOSE WHO LOVE LIFE...NOTICE THE MOMENTS

What have you been waiting to get out of the way before you begin enjoying life more?

Name one thing you intend to notice more.

What is one painful memory you have that changed you and your life for the better—the one from which you've grown the most?

Is there pain now that you're avoiding (or that you are trying to keep from someone else)?

Dr. Gary Schwantz

SOME IDEAS!

- Take a different route home and notice your area as though you were a visitor.

- Go into your backyard and simply watch.

- Do this, pretend you've been sick for a month, unable to get out of the house. All of a sudden, you are well. What is the first thing you would do? Go do that today.

- Think about and share with your kids, your spouse, your parents your favorite moment(s) with them.

- Look on the calendar to note the next full moon. Put together a small picnic basket and go watch it rise somewhere away from the city and the lights.

- Put out a birdhouse or a hummingbird feeder.

Those who Love Life ...

...Celebrate and Have Fun

've told you a little bit about my dad. Let me tell you more. After Janet and I married, we actually lived next door to my folks, out in the country. That was 1984 and at the time, I thought it was a temporary move and actually it was. We only stayed there 15 years and in a moment you'll understand why that wasn't nearly long enough.

Again, I am as surprised as anyone that we lived next to my folks and that we did it well. The pleasure of it was this—my Dad became my best friend. We spent lots of days talking to each other over a short fence that defined our yards. We talked about watering yards (okay, to be honest, I mainly listened while Dad told me how to water my yard) and kids and cars.

In the summer of 1998, we knew my dad had lung cancer and we were doing battle with it. Our conversations took on slightly different tones. The moment I remember most clearly is this one. My dad said to me, "Gary, I wish I'd had more fun." Actually, what he said was this, "Gary, I wish I'd had more fun," then he pointed at me and said, "Like you do!"

My dad was by nature kind, but that was the single kindest and most encouraging thing he ever said to me. Dad died that December and eventually we sold both houses and moved. That's why I say 15 years wasn't nearly long enough. I wish my dad were still around, he would love this fact that I'm writing a book and making a living talking about loving life.

All right, enough of being serious. I don't know the different sources for it, but my wife and I do love to have fun and have made that a focus of our lives from the beginning.

We like cooking and parties and holidays and big celebrations and small ones. For my 50th birthday party, we had a band and invited every person I had ever met (I didn't want to limit to the party to just friends, I mean, what's a party with only 7 people there?) I wrote and performed a song called "Geezer Rap." Perhaps some day I will put it on an album of greatest hits. Can I share with you a couple of my favorite lyrics from the song (please imagine a hip-hop beat).

I drink Metamucil and Citracel
All so my bowels do move well
Or
Be careful of that which does excite us
Can you all say diverticulitis?

Okay, maybe you're not overly impressed. Perhaps you had to be there. The point—we chose to have a party and celebrate. No over-the-hill streamers were allowed, no black balloons. I blew up a copy of my AARP card to poster size and had folks sign in as they came. The fact is, we had great fun and that was the only purpose.

I know plenty of people who choose to ignore birthdays and hate holidays because they don't like the trouble. Dang, I love the trouble. Not too long ago was my wife's 47th birthday. Stealing an idea from a friend who had given his wife 30 gifts for their 30th anniversary, my daughter and I went and bought 47 gifts for my wife (with the generous assistance of the dollar stores in the area). We put each gift in a brown lunch sack and then put a label on each, directing my lovely wife where the next would be found.

Actually, it worked better in theory. By gift number 47, Janet was tired, she had arms full of cheap gifts from the dollar store and a home littered with paper bags. Here's the deal—my daughter and I had a great time buying the gifts and in the years to come, my wife will enjoy the day more in the telling than in the actual experience. Cassidy and I had something to look forward to; we snuck around and coordinated. And Janet has something to reflect on; she knows she is loved—by her daughter and her cheap husband.

SMALL CELEBRATIONS

We do celebrate birthdays in my home. We also celebrate holidays and we love our vacations. But we don't wait for those to have fun. We actually love most the small, everyday celebrations that give life meaning. I think we're good at not waiting for vacations or holidays or even the weekends to have fun and celebrate life.

One of my favorite memories of celebration comes from my nephew Colin, who was four at the time. I loved seeing life through his four-year-old eyes. Remind me to tell you some day of the great fun of watching the movie *Finding Nemo* with him and about 400 other 4-year-olds.

Colin was spending the night with us. He was in another room getting ready for bed and shouted "Uncle Gary, come here, come here!" in an excited voice. I went in. He was standing on the bed—big grin on his face—pointed down and said "Look, Uncle Gary, new underwear!"

His celebratory moment: new Power Rangers underwear and he wanted to share the moment with me. Was that cool or what? As soon as they make Power Rangers underwear in XXL, I may join him!

Celebration...fun...for me, is found in the simplest things. Perhaps not always new underwear (though to be honest, I do celebrate a little bit when I get new underwear). I think this is where a key element of savoring life fits, in tasting and celebrating the simplest aspects of life—noticing them and being grateful and eager for more. It combines the immediacy I mentioned earlier with celebration: notice and enjoy.

Me, I want to choose to savor life. I want to choose perfect days filled with the best of simple things: Arizona Green Tea and Shiner's Bock in the refrigerator, breakfast at a little diner not far from our house, music on my I-Pod while I mow the lawn. Gum in the little antique dishes my wife collects and *Seinfeld* on TV.

In fact, here's what I want you to think about. What can you do to offer yourself a 15-minute vacation? For Janet and me, it's getting in the Miata and going to get frozen custard or taking the dogs for a walk in a different part of our neighborhood or getting a cup of coffee at Starbuck's.

If you want to learn to celebrate, you might want to become a child again, with a new set of eyes. Explore and enjoy. Real freedom means the right to be who you really are. Perhaps simplify your life and lower your expenses.

So, it's confirmed, I like having fun. I like holidays and parties. I also love the weekends, when we can have friends over and cook some slightly different food and enjoy one another. In fact, I could do it every night if I had enough friends and enough food and a wife who wouldn't eventually leave me as a result. I don't want to have to wait for holidays to celebrate—I want to find a way to do it every day, one moment at a time.

BIG CELEBRATIONS AND LITTLE CELEBRATIONS

I already told you that we love celebrations, large and small. I choose to celebrate the big events, and have great fun with them—birthdays and weddings and holidays. But you and I both know that holidays and huge events often bring their own stresses that can overshadow our celebration. That's why I think the real joy in large celebrations are still found in the small pieces that form their structure. Here's what I mean—and I hope I can pull this together well.

Our daughter Cassidy's wedding last year was a beautiful event. But for those of you reading this who have gone through getting a wedding together, you know the actual feeling around the wedding is more relief than anything else. There are always things that go wrong and ways in which the day is not as special as you'd hoped or planned (I'm talking as the parent, not the bride and groom).

The wedding was a real celebration, a wonderful time. But my favorite memories and the real celebrations centered around how close my wife and Cassidy got as they planned this wedding together—a series of small celebrations over a year of planning.

My favorite memory? We were at the bridal shop after Janet and Cassidy had picked out the gown. Cassidy went in to put on the gown and came out and my eyes tear up even now as I think about how excited and beautiful she looked.

See, we chose to make it all a celebration, each tiny piece at a time.

Listen, I love Christmas—the season of Christmas. In fact, as opposed to other geezers, I kind of like the idea that it begins about the day after Halloween. But it is the season I like more than the day itself. At our home, we begin our season by watching *National Lampoon's Christmas Vacation* (sometimes in August). I look forward to stores hauling out decorations.

I think Christmas is real life—a piece anyway. The stress comes from spending too much money and too much time with tradition Nazis who state there is only one way to celebrate Christmas and it must be done in this order and at these times. So my wife and I have tried to be creative. Each year, we decide a limit on what we will buy and the number of gifts we will buy for one another. This past year, the limit was $200 and we had to buy 10 gifts.

One of my favorite friends, Steve Knoll, has a special table with a roll of butcher paper on it. Among his Christmas traditions is buying gifts like toothbrushes and soap (actually, I think he may bring those back from hotels) and wrapping them up in his dedicated roll of butcher paper. That way, everyone in his family has massive numbers of gifts, and though trees give up their life to support his habit, it seems worthwhile. His family gets real gifts also, but it's the ones in the plain brown wrappers that most excite them.

For me, again, life's celebrations and fun are made up of moments, always available and always accessible.

CELEBRATE THE TEMPORARY

I already mentioned the book that had a great influence on me when I was about 19 and working at a camp for the summer down in the Hill Country of Texas. At the time, I had a great Afro and terrible acne—pretty much the sum total of how I perceived myself. The book was *Celebrate the Temporary*, by Clyde Reid. In it, he focused on noticing and celebrating the small things of life. The summer changed me; the sun cleared my skin up (some), the book cleared my perspective up (some), my Afro stayed the same.

Here are a few quotes from his book that have impacted me and that I enjoy sharing:

To celebrate the temporary is to really take time to taste bread and to give it your full attention for just a few minutes. To smell it, touch it, to chew it slowly while it dissolves in your mouth. To think about bread and the life it brings, the strength it gives.

To celebrate the temporary is to lie on your back on the floor, in the dark, and listen, really listen, to a beautiful piece of music. Not doing anything else but listening with every fiber of your being.

To celebrate the temporary is to carry a child on your shoulders instead of walking sedately to the car. To roll with children in the grass and toss them in the air. To celebrate children, who are themselves temporary.

To celebrate the temporary is to get rid of that hairdo that prevents celebrating (author's note: never a problem with an Afro) that can't be rained on or touched or violated by rolling down a hill. To be free of all that self-inflicted bondage is to celebrate the temporary.

Actually, as I type in these pieces from the book, I realize once again how much that little book influenced me to celebrate the simple things. Life is savored in the smell of fresh spices. (Have you ever cooked with fresh ginger?) Or in the unique smell to mornings that I can choose to take in with all my breath.

THE IMPORTANCE OF BEGINNINGS AND ENDINGS

As I write this, we are in the middle of summer. Do you remember what summer felt like as a kid? How the days stretched out and life seemed endless? But as fond as my memories of summer are, more fond is the memory of that great feeling of counting down the days in May, looking to the end of school and the beginning of summer. In fact, I am reminded that one of the things I really enjoyed about life as a kid was a real sense of constant beginnings and endings.

We kids knew it was about time to go back to school when our favorite little shopping center had its sidewalk sale. For us, that was a big day—new pants and shirts—I have no recollection of what shoes we wore; they weren't sneakers. I loved buying school supplies (actually, this is from a guy who never liked school all that much—if you are wondering whether or not the Ph.D. after my name is legitimate, so am I!) Especially vivid was elementary school when we still bought Big Chief tablets and crayons and the colored map pencils that we never used because they were primarily designed to tear holes in any existing paper, all placed proudly in a cigar box.

October brought with it preparations for Halloween. We made those great paper pumpkins of orange and black construction paper, held together by wintergreen-flavored paste. (Don't tell me you didn't suck a little of it down yourself.) We made ghosts of paper bags and white paint. Halloween started that great rush of holidays.

To get ready for Thanksgiving, we made turkeys by tracing around our hand on a piece of brown construction paper and adding construction paper feathers and we learned about the Pilgrims.

Christmas was angels and stars and gifts made of Gerber baby food jars filled with white stones and decorated with construction paper and cotton balls. And Christmas was THE countdown, the countdown to days off from school and Santa Claus. At home, I remember our tall green candle that served as one centerpiece. There was a great miniature Christmas tree made from Styrofoam balls and toothpicks that we re-sprayed every year with artificial snow. And I already told you that I wished my folks had enjoyed putting up the Christmas tree as much as I did.

At church, *The Old Rugged Cross* was replaced by *Away in a Manger* for a season. Christ became a child again, for just a little while, and I honestly could envision that night.

I do remember this also. Nothing ever ended more quickly than Christmas. By about 2:00 that afternoon, it was over. I hated that ending, but moved on.

New Year's was not a kid's holiday; it simply meant going back to school was closer.

Then we hit January, February and March, the only interlude being Valentine's Day, when our teachers were good enough to make certain everyone in the class gave everyone else Valentines but still there were those whose decorated shoeboxes overflowed and others (I'm not speaking of anyone in particular here) whose puny intake of Valentines made him wish the holiday had never existed (again, hypothetically). Let's be frank, Washington's and Lincoln's birthdays and Groundhog's Day didn't do much for us either.

Those early months stretched on endlessly until Easter; when once again Spring seemed like it could appear. Nights got warmer, days longer and the countdown to another summer began.

Forgive the aside, but here's why it matters. I think our life was better and more fun when it had obvious beginnings and endings. I believe that may be what we miss most about being a kid.

Here's our challenge. I'm convinced we need something to look forward to and we need the opportunities to check things off our list. Once we enter "real" life and the workforce, we have very few beginnings and endings. We get a job and it often seems that each day is similar to the previous one. If we do complete another project, there's another to take its place. Every challenge met seems to simply bring another challenge. The sameness wears down our soul and our heart.

What we need, either by design or circumstance, are things to look forward to and things to reflect back on and feel a sense of completion and accomplishment. I think we need to find a way to have beginnings and endings. I can't shut down my job for the summer. Like you, I live in the real world. But I do think there are ways to create and notice those beginnings and endings, ways to tie bows on pieces of life so we notice them.

For those of you who are now saying "Wait a minute! Didn't you just tell us to enjoy the moments, to not spend our entire lives in anticipation!" You're right—I did just say that. But I promise there is no conflict. There is a great pleasure in anticipation, in having something to look forward to. My concern expressed earlier is for those whose entire lives are anticipated, not experienced.

CELEBRATIONS IN BUSINESS

I do a bit of training in companies and also do research on corporate culture and motivation. Dr. Gerald Graham, at Wichita State University, did research into the elements that motivate employees. Here are the top five factors he found:

- The manager personally congratulates employees who do a good job.
- The manager writes personal notes about good performance.

- The organization uses performance as the basis for promotion.
- The manager publicly recognizes employees for good performance.
- The manager holds morale-building meetings to celebrate successes.

Notice first that the primary motivator for employees is personal recognition, is being noticed. But for the purpose of this discussion, notice the importance of celebration. Personal notes, encouragement, public recognition—those are all celebrations of individual accomplishment. Number 5 emphasizes the important of celebrating successes.

Now, let's combine this idea of celebrating Christmas a small piece at a time and celebrating success at work. If I were to wait until the day of Christmas to enjoy the season, I would do two things: put too much pressure on the day itself and limit my enjoyment. If, at work, I celebrate only those major successes, such as earning a bonus, I think I do two things: overemphasize the bonus and underemphasize the other things there are to celebrate, like new customers; someone at work getting married; new products. I am not an expert on this part, but if you are a manager, can you think of ways to celebrate more often?

PASSION!

This is another one of those pieces I know is important and yet, I struggle as to where it goes. Perhaps that's because it is an over-reaching element of savoring life.

My heritage is probably a combination of German, British, perhaps some Scottish, oh yeah, and Baptist. When you think about that combination, does living life with a passion come to mind? Does living with gusto, cooking outrageous meals, being expressive and effusive, come to mind? Nope, I'm working against evolution here.

You know what? I wish I would wake up some morning Italian! I'm pretty sure everything I know about being Italian comes from movies, but I will admit I am envious of the appearance, at least, of living life with a passion.

I will tell you, though, despite the German/British/Scottish/Baptist exterior, I really want to attack life and work with a passion. I want to work with a passion for what I do —or move on. I want to love my wife with a passion. I want to get excited and have people say "Maybe you oughta settle down a bit". Dadgummit, I don't want to settle down! It seems to me that people want passion. Here's what I've found.

I've mentioned my son Patrick a couple of times. Let me tell you what he's taught me about passion. As a kid, Patrick was fairly quiet, didn't get excited about much, or at least didn't share it. I think he inherited, by osmosis, some of my dark side. It wasn't until he happened to take a photography class as an elective that he found his passion.

Now, when he talks about his job as a photojournalist, his eyes light up. He loves the news. Just like all of us, he complains about salary and assignments, but at the heart of it, he loves what he does. It ignites him and in turn, he ignites me. In fact, here's what I'm proudest of. Jobs as photojournalists simply don't pay very well. But he's been strong enough to do what's best (have a job he loves) rather than what's easiest (take a job for the salary, like most others). Here's what else ignites him.

Patrick's wife Brooke is also a photographer, with a wonderful artistic flair! Patrick thinks Brooke is perhaps the finest photographer that he knows; Brooke thinks the same of Patrick. They each believe the other hangs, on a consistent basis, the moon. My greatest answered prayer for my son is a wife he is passionate about and a job he loves. Those passions have opened him up to so many other experiences and to a more optimistic and colorful approach to life.

Find something, anything, you can be passionate about. There are enough people who spend every week with no new sensations, refusing to get overly excited or enthusiastic. Don't be one of them.

FINDING YOUR PASSION

I deal with college students all the time who are making their choices for work based on what a parent or teacher told them they should be doing, not what they want to do. "You're valedictorian of your class; you need to be a doctor." So they follow the wishes and desires of others.

In work situations, people make progress by moving up the ladder, even if that doesn't fit their dreams or passion. I taught with lots of coaches who became administrators, because that's how progress was defined—they loved being a coach, but traded that passion for "progress."

We lose sight of who we wanted to be. We find we owe money on a house and on college and we get addicted to a certain lifestyle. We define progress not by our dreams, but by other standards.

One of my favorite people to visit with and have come into my classes is Andy Wilkinson. Andy spent the first 12 years of his work life as a cop, the next 12 as a stockbroker, but in his heart, he was always a songwriter—a writer and performer of folk and cowboy songs.

As a broker, his goal was to create enough money to allow him to follow his passions. But as he found, the more you earn, the more you spend. And he found that singing and writing on the weekends simply could not sustain that creative urge. Finally, and with the support of the woman he calls an amazing wife, he quit the job and threw himself fully into his passion.

Here's what he tells my students, "You can make a living at anything; it's just how you define making a living." In other words, he got comfortable with the fact that he would be broke but happy. He counted the cost and dove in. I will tell you that he now has several things published, including a couple of plays that are performed all over. He has success and he did it following his passion. But I also know him well enough to know that if he struggled financially from now on, he would be comfortable with it, because he follows his passion.

THOSE WHO UNDERSTAND A THING ARE NOT EQUAL TO THOSE WHO ARE FOND OF IT, AND THOSE WHO ARE FOND OF IT ARE NOT EQUAL TO THOSE WHO DELIGHT IN IT.—CONFUCIUS

Listen, life's short enough as it is, but it is way too short not to choose to have fun and celebrate. It is way too short not to experience passion and adventure and anticipation.

THE IMPORTANCE OF LAUGHTER

One telling statistic, though I'm not sure how accurate the numbers are, is that children laugh an average of 400 times a day. For adults, its about 25. There are indeed reasons to question the accuracy of the statement, but I do know that we could all use a little more laughter in our lives. Laughter activates the chemicals in our bodies that are related to our will to live. Laughter increases our capacity to fight disease and reduces problems associated with high blood pressure, strokes, arthritis, and ulcers. Some research suggests that laughter may also reduce the risk of heart disease.

More importantly, it just feels dang good to laugh. My recommendation to you is — this weekend, commit to watching one silly movie, without apology, and laugh out loud. (You might want to have somebody watch with you, since we actually laugh out loud more when there are others around. Interesting way to communicate, isn't it?) This is all a dramatically philosophical basis to justify watching *Animal House, Dumb and Dumber, Blazing Saddles*, or *National Lampoon's Christmas Vacation*. Tell people you're doing research!

APPLICATION:
THOSE WHO LOVE LIFE...
...CELEBRATE AND HAVE FUN!

What is the last great celebration you had?

When is the next one?

What is the last great celebration you had at work?

When is the next one?

What is one "stupid" movie you will commit to watching within the next 7 days?

What is one fifteen-minute vacation that would work for you?

What is one thing you are truly passionate about—you love doing and time passes slowly when you are doing it?

How are you doing at creating a life that allows you to do that more often—what's holding you back, if anything?

SOME IDEAS!

- Throw a party—it doesn't have to be complex and it doesn't have to have a reason. Set the ingredients out and let people put together their own sliders (small hamburgers) for the grill.

- Splurge a little bit and buy the best cut of meat or the best bread or the best drink you can afford and savor it, really notice it.

- Decorate for the holiday, whatever holiday it is (the weirder the holiday the better – Groundhog Day, for example, or put up your Christmas lights for the weekend (especially if it's July. I know, now I'm getting unreasonable).

- Wear a t-shirt supporting your favorite team (even if it's under your suit).

- Countdown to summer!

- Celebrate your or someone else's birthday.

- In response to your ideas and notes on the previous pages, create the celebration at work.

- Share the passion you described above with someone you trust.

- Life is best celebrated in small things, one at a time. Is there one small thing that really helps you enjoy life (for me, it's frozen custard). Identify it and go do it—this week!

Here is a little exercise in celebration:
I want you to get an album by a young lady named Eva Cassidy. If you can't find one, call me and I will let you borrow mine. The album is entitled *Songbird*. Eva Cassidy died at age 33 of metastatic melanoma. The song is the last one on the album, *Somewhere Over the Rainbow*. The song lasts exactly five minutes. Her voice is genuinely of another world, perfect.

Now, go into a dark room and listen to this one song with no other distractions. Turn it up loud. Celebrate the gifts of the singer and of the songwriter. Savor the words and the tune and that perfect voice. It's a little 5-minute vacation. Take me up on it.

THOSE WHO LOVE LIFE ...
...LET GO

Two vivid memories. I remember when we first dropped Patrick off to begin his college work. We had moved him into his dormitory. Then it was time for band practice for him. We drove over to the band hall, said our good-byes, then watched him walk away, his backpack slung over his shoulders; he didn't look back even once.

My wife and I discussed how much it was like the very first time he got on the big yellow dog (the school bus) to begin kindergarten. He also had a backpack then, he stood tall and brave, ready for his first ride. We did not stand tall and brave. Our stomachs hurt and life had changed.

Six years after that was my daughter. Now my stomach hurt even more, realizing my life would never be the same. In fact, in discussion with several friends we've agreed giving up our daughters to college was actually harder then giving them up to marriage.

My most vivid memory after Cassidy left was going into her bathroom to empty the trashcan. I realized that all the lotions and fragrances and jungle print items would soon be gone, and my stomach hurt a lot.

I know some dads are great about in-depth, life-changing conversations with their kids. That simply was never my gift. What I missed were the momentary pieces: the short conversations and saying good-bye in the morning and good-bye at night as Patrick or Cassidy headed out the door every evening to be somewhere else.

Am I worried about an empty nest? No. Janet and I love spending time together and have been fortunate to build our lives around each other, not our kids. But letting go of both our son and daughter —dang!

Enough rambling. I do believe with all my mind in the phrase "Give your kids roots, then give them wings." My heart, however, needs a little more time.

I find those who love life the most learn the art of release. Somehow they understand that life has its cycles and we spend our life letting go, then holding on once again. I've seen so many different ways in which we let life hold us back because we can't let go. For those of us who are parents, a huge part of loving life is letting go of those kids (while still holding them in our hearts).

WHAT HOLDS US BACK

For some of the guys I went to high school with—back when our classrooms were heated with campfires and we wrote on shovels—for some of them, high school was the peak experience of their lives. They were all-district in football or basketball and dated cheerleaders. They were in the best shape of their lives and believed it would always stay that way. (Fortunately for me, high school was a not a high point of my life. The term "goober" was invented specifically for my place and personality in life. Glasses, braces, bad skin—seriously bad—no athletic skills and I drove a 1965 Rambler Classic American.)

When we high school guys do run into one another, the discussions rarely center on what they are doing now. Instead, it's reminiscing about their old high school days. Or, when it's not, it's discussion of how their kids are replicating their lives for them—all-district football and basketball and dating the cheerleaders. I simply don't get to hear much about them, who they are now.

As I read what I've written, it sounds more critical than it should; I don't mean to be critical. It just seems they never moved on. They couldn't release who they had been (or who they might have been).

We've already discussed pain, but you know how much we struggle because we don't move on from it. Every fall semester, I have kids in the university classes I teach whose "love of their life" ended it that summer. In the dramatic way of those in their twenties, they tell me they will never be able to love anyone again; it's not worth the risk. Fortunately, they are resilient and most will. It's not so easy when you're 25 or 30. You and I both are surrounded by those whose hurt is so deep that they have decided never to take that risk again. Because they cannot release that hurt, because they can't let go, they miss opportunities for deep and affectionate relationships.

DEALING WITH GRIEF

I'm sure you know someone who lost a child or a spouse to an accident or an intentional act. Now I'm into territory about which I have little right to speak, other than as an observer. Here's what I've seen:

The summer I was 16, one of our classmates who could only be described as All-American was killed in a car accident. He was simply one of the most genuine, personable, and talented guys I've ever known. We were all devastated, but no one hurt like his mother. She never got over it, was never able to let go. His room became a shrine and her heart shut down years ago.

Again, I don't have much right to speak and I don't know how I would react, but her bitterness and anguish became a lifestyle, not a process.

On the other hand, I remember vividly being in a courtroom at the end of a murder trial. Two young men had killed a middle-aged man, married with two children. He was delivering stacks of newspapers to make ends meet and they robbed him and then killed him—no reason or purpose.

In Texas, at the end of a trial and sentencing, the victims are allowed to face the killers and say what's on their mind and their hearts. When I was County Commissioner, I would visit the courts at times. Typically, at the end of trials, when the victims have their chance to speak, venom spews. They are enraged, heart-broken and desperate for some satisfaction, some revenge. It breaks my heart for them.

For the trial mentioned, I was able to attend the final day. I didn't know what to expect, but I was floored by what was said.

The now-single mother of two simply faced both of the young men, stated that she was sad for herself and her children. That sadness would always be a part of her life. But then she made what I thought was a life-changing point: that her sadness extended to them also, that she desired to pray for them and that she hoped that this moment would change their lives, positively, forever.

There simply was no oxygen in the room left after she talked. She was not in denial and she did not deny her sadness. This woman happens to work at the fitness center I go to and I can tell you, as a fact, that by the grace of God, she has chosen not to let anger and the need for revenge control her life. She will, she does, live life more abundantly.

It seems to me that those who love life feel their sadness, experience their sadness, but don't use that as the way to define their lives. Again, I have little right to speak on the subject—I simply know what is true because of what I've learned from the examples of others.

FORGIVENESS

Forgiveness is a close relative to release. Listen, my prayer is that I'm never placed in a position where I want revenge. I've seen how it kills a person's spirit and wounds the spirits of all those around. I don't know how I would react. I do know about grudges and how they kill the spirit.

More than ten years ago was my first run for County Commissioner. My main opponent was slightly more right-wing than I (okay, more than slightly). It eventually became a fairly bitter campaign. I won but had plenty of feelings of anger and hurt. I also remember those who had supported me feeding those feelings. I nurtured that grudge to the point where I thought if I ever see this guy in public, perhaps I would pummel him. (I simply like the word "pummel"; actually I'm not sure I'm capable of pummeling anyone). It got so bad I dreaded the thought of seeing him in public.

Eventually, I ran into him at a grocery store. Not entirely comfortable, I nevertheless asked him how he was doing, and he asked the same of me. Life and I moved on. I had harbored a grudge for no value and no purpose. Rather than taking the time and being proactive by inviting him over for coffee, I had given him partial control of my life, a mistake I choose not to make again.

You and I both know that our failure to forgive kills our spirit. In fact, let's forget the fact that perhaps the other person doesn't deserve forgiveness (although I remember the numerical standard in scripture—forgive 7 times 70, after that—you're probably welcome to hold a grudge). Let's forget the fact that they don't deserve forgiveness, you do!

Here's where it gets a little fuzzy. You might ask me, "Gary, how do I let it go?" I respond, "By letting it go." First, whatever it is, stop letting it be the focus of your life. Stop talking about it to everyone you see. If it's a sorry guy you used to be with (let's assume if it was a guy, he was sorry—I'm comfortable with that stereotype), stop hanging around with friends whose primary topic of conversation is how sorry guys are. Instead, hang around people who love their husband (or wife or partners or friends) and let their hope invade your own.

Next, let go of that moment when you know revenge will be sweet, because it won't happen. My greatest enemy in high school was Matt (not his real name). I hated him and he made my life miserable. He was all-district in football, I was all-goober. One day, I would get my revenge. I would be successful and he would be some redneck in a small mobile home. So, fast forward to the 30th reunion several years ago. My basic premise had occurred. I had done okay; he was in a small mobile home, divorced, struggling, and broke. There was no pleasure in meeting again, other than sadness at how small I had become.

If you were anything like me, several girls broke up with you when you were of dating age (I remember on one first date, she said "Gary, I think we're seeing too much of each other" – author's note: very weak humor). Anyway, they would break up and I knew there would be a point where they would come to their senses and beg me back but I would refuse, my dignity and honor intact and theirs in ruins and shambles. A great fantasy and one that never happened— never even came close. But me being the idiot that I am, I held on to it and nursed grudges and tried to arrange situations where we might run into each other (legally, that's called stalking).

Finally, after you stop letting it be the focus of your life and after you stop picturing the moment of revenge, the final piece: focus on the positive. I can't remember if I promised not to preach or not, but if I did, I lied. I'm getting ready to preach. There is great poetry and style and meaning in scripture. One of my favorite pieces, and most meaningful to me, is this:

> *Finally, brethren, whatsoever things are true, whatsoever things are honest, whatsoever things are pure, whatsoever things are lovely, whatsoever things are of good report; if there be any virtue, and if there be any praise, think on these things. Phil 4:8*

So, does anybody really live like that? Doesn't this sound a little juvenile, a little Pollyanna, a little over-optimistic? Yes, it does. So, convince me the other way is better. Convince me that people live lives that are fuller and more meaningful by holding on to their anger and their bitterness. Revenge is not sweet—it kills the spirit and wounds the heart.

I'm not wrong. Focus on those things that are honest and pure and lovely and of good report.

SIMPLY LET GO

All right, I'm done preaching for a while. You know why I don't like a preachy tone? Because it makes it sound like I know how to do it and you don't. Well, let me confess something. I'm not great at letting go. I write these words to remind myself, as much as I am attempting to share my thoughts with you.

Listen, there are so many things we hold on to tightly: our children, our jobs, our past, our anger. I have found that doing so—holding on too tightly— simply limits the life I live now. So, today I will remind myself of what a blessing this current life is and focus on these moments and these blessings.

Schwantz Rant

Can I tell you something to let go of? Let go of your cell phone and laptop computer for two minutes, or maybe even five. Among my colleagues were two interesting guys. Both had similar responsibilities where I worked, with about ten people who report to them (fairly large groups for our organization). I have travelled with both men.

One never had his cell phone or laptop off. His discussions and meetings were constantly interrupted by calls. I have somewhat of a grasp of organizational psychology and I know that he has decided to create a department that cannot function without his constant input. If it were a marriage, we would call it co-dependency: He has to be needed and his staff serve as enablers.

The other guy checks his cell phone at lunch and at the end of the day. First, he's taught his staff to feel comfortable making decisions. Second, he's learned to let go of the phone.

I say this only to make the point that you could choose not to be accessible every moment of every single day. Amazingly, there was a time when we didn't even have cell phones or wireless connectivity. How did we ever manage?

DEBT

When I look at those around me, I find their lives are not usually controlled by their children or their grudges or their dreams. I find their lives are controlled by their debt. They keep jobs they hate because of the debt they created. They buy houses they can't afford. Their driveways are occupied by cars they can't afford. They live from paycheck to paycheck—essentially, they are in bondage. Some make $40,000 a year, some $400,000, yet there is no difference between them. They survive beyond their means, but they are not living and they are not free.

If you (and I) really want to savor life, get rid of debt or the desire to buy. I know it's easier said than done, but here's your goal: Charge only what you can pay off each month. Buy a car that's three years old instead of new. Get a smaller house. Again, easier said than done, but tell me I'm wrong!

Let go of the opinions of others. I love this definition of status: "Buying things you don't need with money you don't have to impress people you don't like."

Real freedom means the right to be who you really are. You want one way to enjoy all you have a bit more? Lower your expenses and simplify your life.

APPLICATION:
THOSE WHO LOVE LIFE...LET GO

Let's think about what is holding you back. Is there a new stage to your life that you need to address? Is it fear and if so, of what? Are there memories (pleasant or unpleasant) that have kept you from moving forward? Is there someone you need to forgive, but haven't been able to? Exactly what words would you say to them to forgive them?

The thing that's been hardest for me to let go of is

I need to forgive_____ and here's why

I need to get rid of:

SOME IDEAS!

- If your children are grown, give them a call. If they are not, then make certain you create some memories this week that means when you are older you let them go with no regrets.

- Tell someone what it is you are finding difficult to let go of – if it is your kids, especially let them know and ask them to help.

- If there is someone you need to forgive, write the script of exactly what you would want to say and put it in your desk.

- If there is someone you need to apologize to, go do it now! I'm serious, set the book down, go find that person, and say "I'm sorry."

- Clean out some closets and get rid of some stuff. Give it away to a favorite charity or thrift shop.

- Spend a day without your phone, your computer and your TV.

- Financially, fast for a week, meaning spend money only on gas and utilities. Otherwise, cook using the food in your pantry and fridge, wear only the clothes you already own, watch movies you already have.

Those who Love Life...

...are Grateful

Actually, the term "grateful heart" probably says it better than just being grateful, because having a grateful heart implies that appreciation is an integral part of our lives.

About a month before my daughter's graduation from high school, her school held an awards ceremony. All students who won an award during that year were invited, along with their parents. We were invited and were excited to see what Cassidy had achieved.

The ceremony was an impressive undertaking. There was a podium up on the stage and the students came up in groups of 15 to stand at the bottom of the stage. As each student's name was called, he or she came up to the podium, the award was announced, the student sat down and the next student came up. After that group of 15 was through, the next group of 15 was waiting at the bottom of the stage. Cassidy's class had about 600 students, yet the school was prepared to recognize every student who had won an award.

Cassidy's group came up. The young lady prior to Cassidy had an impressive resume. She was all-state choir and Academic Decathlon and a winner in several competitions for journalism and Latin and somewhere, I think they mentioned that she adopted abandoned puppies and fed them with eye-droppers until they were strong enough to be given to disadvantaged children (okay, I'm starting to ramble). Anyway, this young lady was up there for literally seven minutes as they named recognition after recognition.

Next up, the light of my life, my daughter—who won an award for what I think was in recognition for having one six weeks straight A report card. That was it—done—move on. The young lady before , 7 minutes; my lovely daughter, about 15 seconds!

I don't know how exactly to best describe how I felt. Ashamed is not the word, but I remember sitting there and somewhere deep inside feeling a bit of discomfort and a bit of jealousy and some embarrassment for my daughter. Why couldn't my daughter be that 7-minute girl? Why does school have to be difficult for her? Cassidy really did work hard in school. Why can't it be easy for her? (Why can't it be easy for me?!?)

Perhaps because I was so focused on Cassidy (actually, I wasn't focused on Cassidy, I was focused on myself), I didn't notice a student in the next group coming up, at least not until he was called up on the stage. His name was Scott and he literally had to pick up one leg and place it on a step so that he could pick up his next leg and do the same. Scott had cerebral palsy, but was still mobile.

He struggled up the steps, struggled across the stage to accept his awards, then struggled down the stage on two legs that could barely support him. I thought how proud Scott's parents must be. Then I suddenly realized how much they might enjoy him being able to simply walk up and off the stage. I don't remember what Scott won—I was too busy wiping tears from my eyes. I wasn't crying for Scott or feeling sorry for him; he was creating a great life. I was crying, I think, for me and why for even a moment I would want my daughter to be anyone besides who she is.

For one sorry moment, rather than listing and counting as blessings all I had in my lovely daughter, I had listed all she wasn't. I had before me a beautiful, intelligent, and healthy daughter and I had failed to appreciate all that meant. For that moment, I had compared her and found her lacking. I had failed to notice and appreciate the wondrous creation of my daughter. This is the daughter we were blessed to adopt exactly one year after my wife had to have a hysterectomy and could bear no more children. This was the daughter who has brought both sunlight and storms into our household. And I, for a moment, had found her lacking. Of course, the only one lacking was me.

Actually, there was a time where I could easily have lost my wife and daughter. Cassidy was six weeks old. We had a little Datsun B210 that Janet drove at the time. Janet was driving on the highway and her right front tire caught the edge of the road. Janet tried to steer it back on to the highway and that sent the car into a spin. The little tin-can of a car evidently spun twice, rolled twice, and ended up in an unhappy introduction to one of the light posts in the median.

I got the call from the police that my wife and daughter had been in an accident, were being transported to an ER, and that both were all right. Amazingly, both were! Cassidy's car seat had done what it was supposed to do. Janet's seat belts had held her in and she had a few bruises, but nothing serious. So, in my mind, "Accidents happen. My wife and daughter are fine. No big deal."

Then I went out to where the rollover had occurred. That's when it hit me. There was glass everywhere. Cassidy's toys were strewn for 50 yards. I have tears now, two decades later, as I think and write about it. Later, I saw what was left of the car—very little. I'm glad I didn't see the crash site first. I would have thought I had lost my family.

Here's the point: I don't know why my wife and daughter were spared. I don't know why there were, I believe, protective angels to save the most precious pieces of my life (as is my son, Patrick). I also don't know why others, much stronger in their faith and life than I, why their families are not protected. At that moment, I promised myself I would never take my family for granted. As you see from the story above, a promise I failed to keep. That is the purpose of intentionality: reminding myself every day of the blessings of this family of my wife, my kids and their spouses.

Here's where being intentional really comes in: in creating and sustaining a grateful heart. Rather than noticing what I don't have or haven't achieved, I slow down and reflect on the great blessings of my life. I have a wife I love with all my heart, and in spite of who I am, she loves me the same. I have a son I admire, who works as a photographer, with great passion, not making much money but doing what he loves. He has a wife whom he believes hung the moon; she the same for him. I have a daughter who lights up a room and fills my heart. She is married to a young man who I think understands her spirit and her needs, takes her seriously without taking her too seriously. I have a home I love and friends who surround it.

Who am I not to be grateful? All I know is that I am grateful, genuinely grateful, every day that all those wonderful people are a part of my life.

Sometimes my job is not perfect, but who am I not to be grateful?

At times, I am frustrated with every member of my family above mentioned, singularly and/or jointly, but who am I not to be grateful?

At times, just like you, I feel like I don't have a single friend or a single talent, but who am I not to be grateful?

I know my life is better when I list and count and note my blessings. I wonder what blessing I might lose today that would make me wish I had my old life back? I worked in an industry that provides equipment for those with disabilities, many who were walking one day and were not the next. How much would I miss my life now and realize how I had taken it for granted if my legs no longer functioned and I could no longer take my dogs for a walk or drive my little car with its standard transmission or stroll around in my backyard?

If I lost my son, my daughter or my wife, how much would I wish I had told them I loved them more often or that I admire and adore them and thank God for them each day?

So, I remind myself every day that my blessings are gifts, not entitlements. I love this quote from Maya Angelou about having "the ability to take delight in small offerings, an assurance that the world owes you nothing, and that every gift is exactly that—a gift."

I will choose not to compare myself to others. Instead of envying the cars and homes and achievements of others, I will work to delight in them and encourage them and be glad for them.

> Speaking of comparisons and "keeping up with the Joneses," here is a great quote from Lucy Grealy, author of *Autobiography of a Face*: "Society is no help. It tells us again and again that we can most be ourselves by acting and looking like someone else."

I will also not compare others unfavorably to myself. It kills my spirit, primarily because I begin to feel superior and think that somehow I earned these blessings God gave me. I did not. Instead I will count my blessings, name them one by one, in reflection. If I want to savor life, I will do it slowly and with a grateful heart and an attitude that seeks the positive.

I love the perspective from this piece by Philip Gulley in his collection of writings called *Front Porch Tales*.

My mother was the first to notice how our son Spencer's feet and nose pointed in different directions when he walked. We took him to the bone doctor, who laid our one-year-old on a table and looked him over.

"Your son has turned-in feet and a hernia," he informed us. "The feet we can fix with arch supports, but he'll need an operation for the hernia."

Surgery was scheduled for the following day. I called Mom to tell her the news. She reminded me that hernias were a family tradition. My younger brother David had one when we were little and shared a bedroom. I remembered.

Mom and Dad had called the kids together.

"David will need an operation," they told us.

"Could it kill him?" my sister asked.

"We never know," Dad said, "so we'd better pray."

I prayed, but not too hard, since I'd always wanted a bedroom of my own. David not only survived, he came home from the hospital with the neatest toys. His was the perfect childhood illness— serious enough to merit presents, but not so painful he couldn't play with them.

With Spencer's surgery, everything came out fine. The arch supports did the trick, and the half-hour surgery was text book. Even the scars went away.

Blessed is the family whose gravest problems are so easily remedied. A cousin of mine gave birth some years ago. A long-faced doctor came out and told her that her son had three holes in his heart. It tore a hole in her heart, too. Some scars are a long time healing.

One thing I've never understood is why I'm so blessed—good parents, good wife, good kids, good job—and others aren't. I used to think it was because I was nice to God, until I met some battered saints. Now I just think there's a randomness in this world beyond my understanding—on this side of things we see in a mirror dimly.

If you woke up this morning and your kids were healthy and your parents loved you, then you don't have any problems. You might think you do, but you don't. And if at night, when you steal into your child's room and watch that little body rise and fall with the breathing, and your heart aches with love, consider your life sublime.

My question to you (and me) is "What have you been taking for granted lately?"

APPLICATION
THOSE WHO LOVE LIFE ... ARE GRATEFUL

The one thing I take most for granted is:

The person I know who really has a grateful heart is

If it were taken away from me today, the thing I would most miss is

Here's your assignment. Get a piece of paper and make two columns. In the left-hand column, I want you to write down 5 things for which you are grateful. Off the top of your head.

Now, here's what I want you to do next. Get really specific. In the right-hand column, for example, if you said you are grateful for your wife, put down something specific. Is it her kindness to older people, her laugh, her cooking? If it's your health, get more specific. What do you enjoy most about your health, being to bike every now and then or is it simply being able to walk without having to use oxygen?

For each item, get very specific. Now take a moment and read those out loud and note your gratitude.

Dr. Schwantz's prescription: Do this every day, with five different items, for one month. Honestly, what would happen if you were to do what I suggest? Spend time each morning counting 5 specific blessings, writing them down and posting them on the wall?

THOSE WHO LOVE LIFE...
... TAKE TIME

I heard a motivational speaker, Jeff Conley, at a banquet few years ago. Jeff made several great points in his presentation, but the one that stuck with me most is the competition between SPEED v. SPIRIT in our lives. His simple point was: the faster we move, the less we can tend to and nurture our spirits.

Reflection is difficult to do at 70 mph, with ZZ Top pounding in your ears, while talking to your daughter on the cell phone (as I did this morning). Reflection, I believe, requires us to slow down and rest and be quiet (scripture talks about a still, small voice).

Do you think technology has improved our lives or damaged them? (Actually, this is a rhetorical question, a favorite of we professorial types. You already know the answer I'm going to offer; there's really no need to respond).

If you are my age, you remember having one big, black phone and getting an extension was a major technological breakthrough. You remember the first pocket calculator from TI that did addition, subtraction, division and multiplication, all for the low, low cost of about $200! You remember life before the microwave and when we had TVs with two big knobs and the only remote control was us, the 8-year-olds.

Now we have cell phones, pocket computers that are more powerful than those on Apollo 11, microwave/convection ovens, on-line banking, and home theatre systems with 7 remotes and 118 channels. (Actually, to be honest, home theatre systems are ordained in scripture—I don't want anyone messing with those).

So, with all of these "conveniences," are you more relaxed? Do you feel more at peace in a world where you can take work with you 24 hours a day, where you can always be reached by phone? The reality is that we work more hours than we ever have and take less lei-sure time.

You know that we've done the same thing to our kids. They are over-organized and over-scheduled. I have friends who don't have a single night open because their kids are doing something every min-ute: soccer, ballet, theatre, baseball, basketball. Eventually, they got into a rhythm where doing any less doesn't feel right. In fact, we all do.

We move so quickly and so often that we think the speed at which we move is the speed for which we are built. Well, we are wrong. Maybe you don't know it, but your body knows that you are not intended to always travel at 5,000 rpm and eventually, it will let you know.

BREATHING

Reflection is an intentional approach to slowing down and noticing life. Here's one easy way to so do—breathe deep. We tend to use only the upper part of our lungs in breathing. We breathe shallowly and at times, live shallowly. Breathing deeply is how we literally can come to our senses.

Do you even remember, a little bit, what it feels like to be relaxed? Here is a reminder of what it feels like. Right now, simply inhale as deeply as you can and hold it for a moment. Do nothing else but breathe deeply. Physiologically, your heart rate will slow because it doesn't have to try so hard to get oxygen to your blood.

Now, notice some of what is going on around you—the smells and the sights. Don't think about what you have to get done today, just notice.

This is one of those areas where I dramatically fail to practice what I preach. Even as I am writing this about breathing, I'm not willing to slow down and do what I am saying at this very moment: simply breathe. In my primitive brain, I'm convinced I am breathing correctly and keep on working. I'm an idiot. So, here's what I'm going to do. As I write, it is early morning. I'm going outside, right now, and breathe. I know I need to finish this section, but I will go breathe. It goes against my nature; that's why it is a good idea...

...I'm back. I did take some deep breaths and worked to exhale some of the stress under which I'm putting myself. I'm not very good at it. This is a reminder that you are working here with someone from the dark side. I know what I need to do; practice is my challenge (and perhaps yours as well).

IT IS THE JOURNEY

There are two things I love doing: building and cooking. And, in fact, it is with those activities that I have best realized another important element of savoring life: it really is the journey, not the destination. How many times have you heard that or read it on a poster? Just because it's been repeated so many times doesn't make it any less true. Now, here's where I'm at on this journey in my life.

When I am cooking the right way, here's what happens. I let my creative spirit take over and simply enjoy the whole journey. I turn on the music real loud. I get every ingredient out. I take out every bowl and utensil that I'll need, and prepare for the food symphony. I chop the vegetables and put them in individual bowls as though I were Emeril (bam!). Have you ever used fresh ginger in a dish? It's very cool! I smell the smell of onions simmering. If I'm making bread, I take pleasure in kneading the dough. Somehow I get into a zone where I notice and experience everything I'm doing. I don't think about when I will be done, instead I simply enjoy the moment. That's creation.

Done right, I honestly do feel like I'm an artist and the food is my art.

When I do it wrong, I put myself on a false time limit (sometimes it's a real time limit, meaning I should have started earlier). In those cases, cooking is not something I GET TO do, it's something I've GOT TO do. I no longer enjoy it. It's a chore. I'm certainly no artist, just a short-order cook. I stop enjoying the journey and simply look to the finished product, a meal on the table.

Being on the journey is even more prevalent in my life when I'm building something. I can't tell you how many times I've been halfway to building some bookcases and thinking "You know, if I hurry I can finish by this afternoon!" Then I drive myself to get that much done. If I screw up, my plan is ruined, I get frustrated, and I throw a drill or two (I decided not to toss any more saws, or at least I turn them off before I throw them).

The real issue here is: what's the rush? What's wrong with me? I created an artificial timeline to get something done that I originally thought I was doing for fun. Again, welcome to my dark side!

Instead, I now focus on enjoying the journey. I enjoy the smell of the wood as I saw it. I take care to put it together just right. In the past, I would try to take shortcuts to put it all together. Now, instead, I'm more careful to prepare. In carpentry, there are several jigs you can build to make your job easier in the long run. It takes more time to do this in the beginning, but saves time and effort later in the project. I work to do a better job of thinking about and laying out the tools I need—before I begin. And when the work is done well, I view myself as an artist (and a carpenter).

REFLECTION AND BEGINNING THE DAY

Our days are dramatically impacted by how we begin them. Allow me to share this piece I borrowed from a friend, Claude Dollins, with his permission. It's called *Saddlin' Up Time* and describes so much better than I can how to begin the day.

> My dad was a cowboy—we called him "Rope." Like most young boys, I loved spending time with Rope. As I look back, I recall an experience that was most meaningful to me. My dad was an early riser. He was up most mornings before the sun, drinking coffee, getting ready for the day.
>
> On several occasions, I remember one scene that made a valuable impact on my life. The scene took

place at the barn. Cowboys call it "saddling-up time."

Some of the things I remember about saddling-up time:

He would very slowly walk up to his horse, speaking in a low, soft voice.

He would gently slip the bridle over the ears of the horse and allow the horse to take the bit. This was the first contact of the day and it was slow and gentle.

Carefully and patiently, he would brush the horse with even and gentle strokes, talking in a subdued voice to the animal as he moved from side to side.

With ease and little motion, he would gently slide the blanket on the back of the horse, always reassuring the animal.

Next, with one motion, he would place the saddle on the horse, walking around the horse to make certain all girths and cinches were in place.

The final step in this slow, deliberate and intentional process, was to take the reins and turn the horse 360 degrees to check one last time before mounting to be sure everything was ready and in place for the day's work.

With precision, he would put his left foot in the stirrup and with one movement, with ease and grace, he would place his hand on the saddle horn and pull himself into the saddle.

A you read those words, did you notice some of the keys to beginning a day effectively? Words like "gentle," "slowly," "intentional." As the first hour of the day goes, so goes the day.

Effective saddling up encourages:

- A daily routine
- Being quiet
- Being intentional
- No rush
- Being awake
- Paying attention
- Clear focus
- Positive habits
- Common sense
- Enjoyment

Assess your morning routine.

- Do you allow yourself to enter the day with ease?

- Do you observe a "quiet" time to focus on what's important?

- Does your early morning routine get you positive results throughout the day?

APPLICATION:

THOSE WHO LOVE LIFE.. TAKE TIME

If you chose to take time this week to do anything you wanted to do, what would that be and what is keeping you from taking that time?

If you could change the way you begin your days, how would you?

What renews your spirit – and I mean something you can access on a daily basis?

Some Ideas!

- Identify one thing you would love to do more of to relax—where you enjoy the journey. Do it.

- This Sunday, sit down with some cookbooks and pull together the menu for the entire week—get creative. Go shopping, post the menu on your fridge. Notice how much easier life is when you get organized to allow creativity.

- When you find yourself getting frustrated, slow down and breathe, count your blessings, and go for a walk.

- For one week, commit to getting up 30 minutes earlier. Use those thirty minutes as described above—for saddlin' up time.

Final Thoughts

Tuesdays with Morrie

There are times when authors simply get it right. Actually, there are times they get it perfect. I've never read a passage that better states what I wish I were able to say about immediacy and enjoying the small things in life.

Let me share with you this piece I love from the book, *Tuesdays with Morrie*, by Mitch Albom. If you haven't read it, I think you would enjoy it very much. It's the true story of Mitch's weekly visits with his former professor and mentor, Morrie, as the latter died slowly from ALS. This exchange is at the very end of Morrie's life, when he is unable to move at all and relies on a respirator to survive.

Tell me he doesn't hit the perfect tone here. It begins with this question from Mitch, with Morrie answering:

> "What if you had one day perfectly healthy?" I asked. " What would you do?"
>
> "Twenty-four hours?"
>
> "Twenty-four hours."
>
> "Let's see...I'd get up in the morning, do my exercises, have a lovely breakfast of sweet rolls and tea, go for a swim, then have my friends come over for a nice lunch. I'd have them come one or two at a time so we could talk about their families, their issues, talk about how much we mean to each other. Then I'd like to go for a walk, in a garden with some trees, watch their colors, watch the birds, take in the nature that I haven't seen in so long now.
>
> "In the evening, we'd all go together to a restaurant with some great pasta, maybe some duck—I love duck—and then we'd dance the rest of the night. I'd dance with all the wonderful dance partners out there, until I was exhausted. And then I'd go home and have a deep, wonderful sleep."

"That's it?"

"That's it."

It was so simple. So average. I was actually a little disappointed. I figured he'd fly to Italy or have lunch with the President or romp on the seashore or try every exotic thing he could think of. After all these months, lying there, unable to move a leg or foot— how could he find perfection in such an average day?

Then I realized that was the whole point.

Here's why that story hits the perfect note. We've discussed several elements of those who savor life, of those who see life as a "GET TO."

- They do it on purpose
- They notice the moments
- They celebrate and have some fun
- They let go
- They are grateful
- They take time

In that simple story is a reflection of all we've discussed. In Morrie, I see a man who defined his life on purpose. He sees and notices the moments—the trees, colors and birds. He celebrates life. He dances and loves his food (at least in his memory). If you've read the book, you see a man who let go of what his body used to be and now deals with it as it is, who feels no self-pity. He is a man with a grateful heart, who wants to spend his time with his friends. He is simplicity itself. Finally, you can see in his responses that he, even with only 24 hours, would take life slowly and experience fully the entire day.

What is my, Gary Schwantz's, prayer right now?

"God, give me the grace and wisdom to find perfection in such an average day."

APPLICATION:

THOSE WHO LOVE LIFE …

- Do it on purpose
- Notice the moments
- Celebrate and have fun
- Let go
- Are grateful
- Take time

My final task for you is this: Describe your perfect day, but keep it within 30 minutes of your home. How would the day begin, who would be there? What's for breakfast? What's next? Where would you go? What's for lunch and where will you have it? How would you spend the afternoon? How does the afternoon end? Who accompanies you for dinner and what happens afterward? How will it feel to hit the bed—will there be music playing?

Write it up and share your ideas with someone you care about, and someone who cares about you.

Epilogue

hank you for journeying through this book with me. Please, if you enjoyed what you read, would you let me know? More importantly, if you tried some of the ideas, would you share them?

I would love to hear about you special weekends, your time with family, your favorite stupid movie, music that moves you. My email is gary@drgaryschwantz.com

I look forward to hearing from you.
Best wishes, Dr. Gary Schwantz

ABOUT THE AUTHOR

D r. Gary Schwantz has a Ph.D. in Family and Consumer Sciences Education from Texas Tech University. His focus in those studies was adult education and customer service in industry and education. His master's is from University of North Texas in Public School Administration and bachelor's from Texas Tech—Family Studies and Home Economics Education.

Gary is now a full-time speaker and facilitator, and some would even say humorous and inspiring. (Unfortunately, people have not yet been willing to write that down—they would only state he was humorous and inspiring off the record).

Dr. Schwantz was most recently Director of Educational Services for The MED Group, and spent seven years creating courses and facilitating programs for the group. He has also completed his 10th year as faculty in the College of Human Sciences at Texas Tech University and twice has received recognition as Outstanding Faculty. At the University, Gary has taught courses in Interpersonal Skills, Law in the Hotel/Restaurant Industry, and now teaches a course entitled Human Sciences Seminar. Each semester, he teaches two sections of the Seminar with more than 150 students in each section.

Gary's careers have spanned a number of industries: high school teacher and administrator; administration in community college; carpenter and remodeling contractor; ministry; grant development for a hospital; even County Commissioner for Lubbock County (and even more surprising, actually re-elected!)

Gary's real highlights are his wife, Janet, a speech pathologist; his son, Patrick, employed as a photographer with the paper in San Angelo, Texas, and Brooke, Patrick's perfect match; and his daughter, Cassidy, finishing up nursing school at Angelo State, married to her perfect match, Sly Luna, who is finishing up his degree in education. Gary also has two greyhounds, both he is dramatically fond of, in spite of their bad breath and shedding.

If you would like to contact Dr. Schwantz, or are interested in having him speak to your group, he would be thrilled to visit with you. His information is:

Dr. Gary Schwantz
3015 21st St.
Lubbock, TX 79410
Tel: 806.283.4193
Email: gary@drgaryschwantz.com
Website: www.drgaryschwantz.com

Thank you!